KNOLE

Kent

Robert Sackville-West

THE NATIONAL TRUST

Acknowledgements

This new guidebook has been written by Robert Sackville-West.
The tour chapter draws heavily on the previous edition written
by Gervase Jackson-Stops, on Natalie Rothstein and Santina
Levey's report on the furnishing textiles, on comments from
Alastair Laing, and on recent research on Knole and its collections
managed by John Chesshyre and John Coleman. The majority of
the family portraits are reproduced by kind permission of Lord
Sackville. Virginia Woolf's *Orlando* is published by the Hogarth
Press © The Estate of Virginia Woolf, for which the Society of
Authors is Literary Representative. We have tried, and failed, to
find the copyright owner for Graham Sutherland's portrait of the
5th Lord Sackville. The National Trust is also very grateful to the
following for their help: Dr David Bostwick, Kate Bosley, the
Centre for Kentish Studies in Maidstone, Ruth Gofton, Mr Tomalin,
Peter Mandler, Rosemary and Peter Milton-Thompson,
Dr Rosalind Murrell, Anthony Wells-Cole, Christopher Wood.

Oliver Garnett

Photographs: British Library p.88; John Coleman p.87; Courtauld
Institute of Art pp.71, 82; Brian Delf pp.6–7; Centre for Kentish
Studies, Maidstone pp.52, 53; Mancktelow Photography pp.5, 67;
National Trust pp.73 (left), 90, 91, 92; NT/David Sellman p.93;
National Trust Photographic Library pp.22, 72, 94; NTPL/John
Bethell pp.45, 50; NTPL/Andreas von Einsiedel front cover, pp.1,
11, 12, 15, 17, 19, 21, 25, 27, 28, 30, 31, 33, 35, 37, 39, 40, 41, 43, 60,
61, 73; NTPL/John Hammond pp.13, 18, 26, 48, 49, 57, 68 (left),
69, 74, 75, 77, 79, 80, 81, 84, 85; NTPL/Angelo Hornak p.83;
NTPL/Horst Kolo pp.24, 36, 71; NTPL/Geoffrey Shakerley
pp.63, 65, 66, 68 (right); NTPL/Ian Shaw p.8; NTPL/Rupert
Truman pp.9, 10, 47, 51, 55, 58; Victoria & Albert Museum Picture
Library back cover; Christopher Wood Gallery p.44.

First published in Great Britain in 1998 by the National Trust

© 1998 The National Trust

Reprinted with revisions 1999, 2000; reprinted 2003

Registered charity no.205846

Designed by James Shurmer

Phototypeset in Monotype Bembo Series 270
by SPAN Graphics Ltd, Crawley, West Sussex (SG1284)

Print managed by Centurion Press Ltd (BAS)
for the National Trust (Enterprises) Ltd,
36 Queen Anne's Gate, London SW1H 9AS

(*Front cover*) The late 17th-century silver furniture in the
King's Room

(*Title-page*) The Sackville leopard on the Great Staircase

(*Back cover*) Lady Betty Germain's China Closet about 1880;
by Ellen Clacy (Victoria & Albert Museum)

CONTENTS

THE SPIRIT OF KNOLE

Knole has always excited a range of different re-actions. Henry VIII liked it so much that he forced Thomas Cranmer, his Archbishop of Canterbury, to hand it to him in 1538. And yet, the following century, the diarist John Evelyn was so depressed by the greyness of this 'greate old fashion'd house' that he hurried out into the sunshine. In the 18th century, Horace Walpole was impressed by Knole's 'beautiful decent simplicity which charms one', but on a later visit decided that it 'has neither beauty nor prospects.'

These mixed emotions can partly be explained by the many faces Knole presents on different days and at different times of the year. On a dull winter's day, as you ride the crest of the knoll in front of the house, and the north front looms in sight, Knole's sprawling mass of sodden Kentish ragstone strikes a sombre note. But on a sunny summer's day, the south front – with its colonnade of seven lightly coloured marble arches – dances to a very different tune.

Vita Sackville-West had grown to love Knole's many faces from her happy childhood here. In *Knole and the Sackvilles* (1922), she wrote that Knole 'has a deep inward gaiety of some very old woman who has always been beautiful, who has had many lovers, and seen many generations come and go'. Vita also believed that the house had grown organically and that it was still very much a living organism. 'It is above all an English home,' she continued, 'It has the tone of England; it melts into the green of the garden turf, into the tawnier green of the park beyond, into the blue of the pale English sky.'

However poetic the description, it is not strictly true. For Knole and its magnificent collection of furniture, paintings and textiles have not grown organically, or indeed continuously. The family's occupation of Knole was interrupted by the Civil War in the 17th century, by residence near the Court in London, and by spells abroad in public office during the 18th century. Even when the family were at Knole, by the end of the 17th century they had withdrawn to private apartments on the ground floor and tended to live there rather than in the more formal, public rooms on the first floor – today's show rooms.

Knole was rebuilt and then furnished in three main bursts of activity, each separated by around a hundred years. In the early 17th century, Thomas Sackville, 1st Earl of Dorset transformed a late medieval archbishop's palace into a Renaissance mansion. Towards the end of the 17th century, his great-great-grandson, the 6th Earl, acquired Knole's unique collection of Stuart furniture and textiles through his office as Lord Chamberlain. And then, towards the end of the 18th century, the 6th Earl's great-grandson, the 3rd Duke, added Old Masters bought on the Grand Tour to Italy and portraits commissioned from contemporary English artists such as Reynolds and Gainsborough.

The visitor today sees a house and collection little changed since the 3rd Duke's day. The very fact that large areas of Knole were inhabited only intermittently from the end of the 17th century, and that the furniture therefore remained under dust sheets for long periods, accounts for its miraculous survival. That is what is so extraordinary about Knole – and what can make the house difficult to understand or appreciate at first. It has been a show house ever since Thomas Sackville's day.

Visitors expecting the exquisite all-of-a-piece integrity of a Kedleston, or the intimate upstairs-downstairs domesticity of an Uppark or Erddig, will be disappointed. But take Knole on its own terms, and you might grow to love the fading magnificence of a house that, like the gilding on its paintings, smoulders rather than sparkles.

A dinner in the Great Hall given by Lionel, 2nd Lord Sackville (with the white beard in the centre on the left-hand side of the table) for officers of the West Kent Yeomanry in May 1904. The girl with her hair down at the near end of the table is the twelve-year-old Vita Sackville-West. The artist, Charles Essenhigh Corke, has pasted photographs of the heads to his watercolour

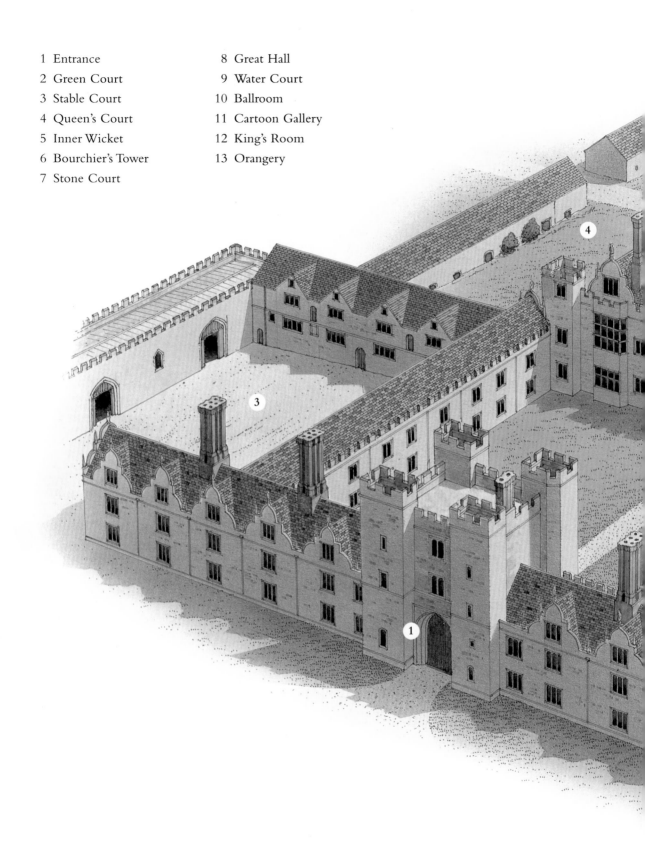

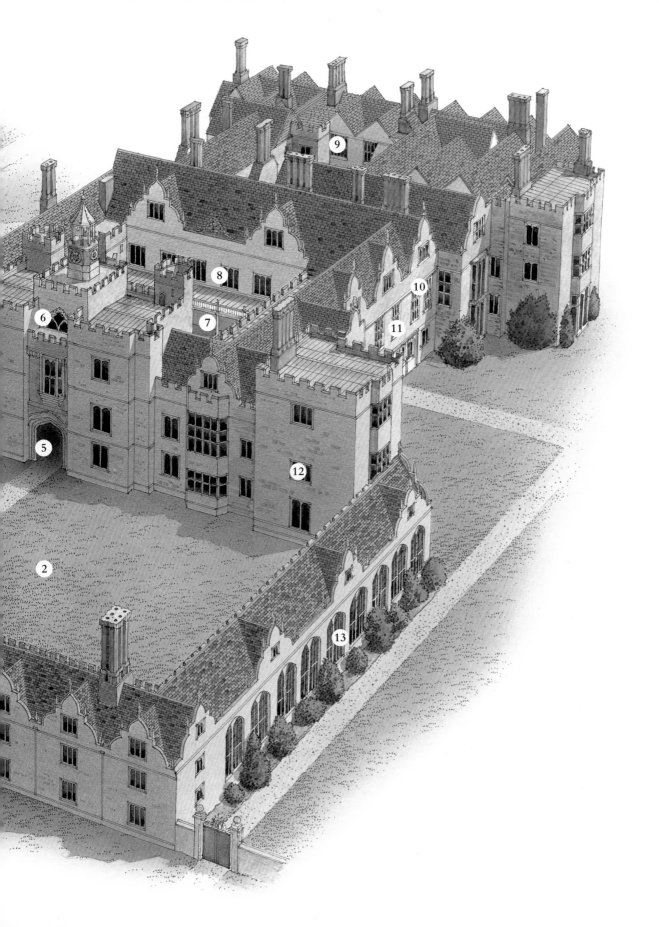

CHAPTER ONE

TOUR OF THE HOUSE

The Approach

THE WEST FRONT

'A beautiful, decent simplicity which charms one', wrote Horace Walpole of the plain, almost demure, west front facing the park, which gives little hint of what will gradually unfold, once the main gateway has been passed.

The central gatehouse, with its four battlemented corner turrets, and the rest of this front were almost certainly built by Henry VIII between 1543 and 1548, to provide the additional lodgings necessary for his retinue. The groups of six octagonal brick chimneystacks, placed at irregular intervals, were part of his work, though the window surrounds seem to date from the early 17th century, when the curved gables surmounted by the heraldic Sackville leopard were probably added by Thomas, 1st Earl of Dorset. The Sackville and Cranfield arms in the spandrels of the entrance arch were added by the 6th Earl in the late 17th century.

THE OUTER WICKET

A beadle's mace can be seen in the outer gateway, known as the Outer Wicket, together with a black-painted 16th-century Italian *cassone*, or chest, a pair to that in the King's Closet. The large Gothick hanging lantern dates from the early 19th century.

The west front

Bourchier's Tower in the Green Court

THE GREEN COURT

This is the largest of the seven courtyards at Knole. The three lower ranges, of only two storeys, were probably built, like the Base Court at Hampton Court Palace, to lodge Henry VIII's attendants, which would explain the large number of doorways and small windows, giving almost the appearance of almshouses. The range on the left, as you stand facing the inner gatehouse, is still known as the King's Stables (although only used as such after Henry VIII's time); while that on the right was converted into an orangery, with large Gothick windows facing on to the garden, by Lord Whitworth in 1823.

The higher three-storey range directly opposite the outer gate is considerably earlier, however, and was the original west front of Archbishop Bourchier's mid-15th-century building, to which Henry VIII simply tacked on an outer courtyard. The façade is again austere, with a minimum of decoration, mostly concentrated in the central oriel window of the great inner gatehouse, known as Bourchier's Tower. Either side of the oriel are machicolations, or openings between corbels supporting a projecting parapet: they are, in fact, survivals from an age when it might have become necessary to pour boiling water or molten lead upon the heads of assailants, but were here used purely for decoration.

Much of the stonework here, as elsewhere at Knole, has had to be replaced during a 20-year programme of restoration, begun in 1963 and generously supported by the Historic Buildings Council.

Apart from the oriel, only the topmost windows in the recessed corners of the gate-tower remain unchanged from Archbishop Bourchier's period. The two projecting bay windows with shaped gables above them, decorated with obelisks and surmounted by the Sackville leopard, were added by the 1st Earl in 1605, perhaps designed by John Thorpe, the master mason and surveyor who did much work for him at Buckhurst, the Sackville house in Sussex. Of the other windows on this front, some are early 16th-century and the others were enlarged in the early 19th century. At the corners of the façade are two castellated towers: that on the right, known as the King's Tower, is more massive than the other and was probably added to the original structure, perhaps by Arch-

The Stone Court

bishop Morton, Bourchier's successor, between 1487 and 1500, and enlarged by the 1st Earl in 1603–8.

The low central turret of the gatehouse, set back above the oriel, was built about 1745 by the 1st Duke, to support the clock which originally stood on the roof of the Great Hall. But its large arched window with Gothick tracery is probably still later, added by Earl Whitworth early in the 19th century.

CLOCK

The bell on which the hours are struck was cast in 1540 by Jan ter Steghe at Kampen in the Netherlands, probably for Henry VIII, who had acquired Knole two years earlier. The inscription on the bell may be freely translated: 'St George is my name: may my sound be pleasing to God.'

SCULPTURE

IN CENTRE OF LAWNS:

The two lead statues are casts of the *Borghese Gladiator* and *Venus rising from the Bath*, placed here by the 3rd Duke in the late 18th century.

The groin-vaulted lobby under Bourchier's Tower is known as the Inner Wicket, and leads to the Stone Court.

THE STONE COURT

This court takes its name from the large flagstones. Beneath these is a reservoir of water, filled by the rain-water coming down from the gutters: this, apparently, supplied the drinking-water to the house from at least the days of the 1st Earl, although before this it was probably drawn from a well in the third courtyard, beyond the hall range, still known as the Water Court.

The Stone Court offers a particularly interesting illustration of the way in which Knole has grown. Several centuries are here represented. There is Bourchier's work of the late 15th century, then there is the addition of the gables and the Doric colonnade by the 1st Earl in the early 17th century, and finally the balustrade surmounting it, covered in moulded lead, which bears the initials of Lionel, 1st Duke of Dorset and the date 1748. In the centre of the parapet, above the balustrade, is a carved stone cartouche with the arms of Cranfield, flanked by festoons of fruit and flowers; it was brought to

Knole from Copt Hall, the Cranfield house in Essex, after it was sold by the 6th Earl in 1701. The 20th century is represented by the complete rebuilding, in 1982–3, of the east wall, made necessary by the deterioration of the fabric and the gradual bowing-out of the structure.

The tower to the right as you look back at the Inner Wicket is known as Shelley's Tower. This is a corruption of the surname of Giovanna Baccelli, the Italian mistress of the 3rd Duke, who had rooms in this tower, and whose name the English servants could not properly pronounce.

RAIN-WATER PIPES

The lead heads of the rain-water pipes bear the initials T.D. (Thomas Dorset), and the date 1605; no two pairs are alike. The rain-water pipes themselves are secured to the wall by lead plaques of fine workmanship, ornamented with the Sackville coat of arms surrounded by the ribbon of the Garter, and flanked by the ubiquitous leopard.

SCULPTURE

SET INTO WALL BEHIND COLONNADE:

Alabaster relief of a sea-monster entwining a mandolin-playing putto. It is based on an engraving in Jacob Floris's *Veelderhande cierlijke Compertementen* (1564).

Four plaster casts by John Flaxman, two of which are models for part of the frieze of the Covent Garden theatre, designed by Robert Smirke in 1808. Smirke's theatre burnt down in 1855, but the frieze was incorporated into the present building.

The collection of antlers includes a pair of prehistoric elk horns excavated in Co. Dublin and presented to the 1st Duke in the early 18th century.

The Antique marble busts were bought by the 3rd Duke in Italy during his Grand Tour in 1769. The plinths originally stood in the Cartoon Gallery and were decorated by Mark Antony Hauduroy, whose work on the Second Painted Staircase and in the King's Room was paid for in 1723–4.

LEFT OF DOOR:

An 18th-century wrought-iron shop sign.

The arched doorway under the colonnade on the left leads into the Screens Passage.

The Interior

THE SCREENS PASSAGE

The two doors on the left of this passage originally served the buttery and pantry, while the great kitchen lay beyond, through the door at the far end of the passage. The fact that the kitchen was a separate building (along the north side of the Water Court) is evidence of the grand scale on which Archbishop Bourchier's original 15th-century house was built.

The two doors on the right of the passage lead into the Great Hall.

THE GREAT HALL

This room was built about 1460 as part of Archbishop Bourchier's house, but practically all that remains of that period are the two stone doorways at the far (south) end.

It was much altered between 1605 and 1608 by the 1st Earl, who put in the plasterwork ceiling and the much ornamented oak screen.

The richly carved screen in the Great Hall was designed by William Portington, the King's carpenter

EATING IN THE HALL

A list of seating arrangements for meals at Knole between 1613 and 1624 suggests that by that date the family usually ate in private upstairs and the senior servants in the Parlour. The Great Hall was used by the household and estate servants, with the steward presiding. The middle-ranking servants, such as the Master Cook and the Yeoman of the Pantry, sat at the Clerks' Table, the lower servants (who included a barber and a bird-catcher) at the long table which still survives here. Other tables were set aside for the Nursery, Laundry and Kitchen and Scullery staff.

When members of the family were present, they would have occupied a table on the raised dais at the far end of the room, afterwards retiring through the small door at the right which leads to the Parlour.

At meals and dances, the 1st Earl's private orchestra would have often performed in the minstrels' gallery behind the lattice windows in the upper part of the screen.

SCREEN

The screen was probably carved by William Portington, who was master carpenter to both Elizabeth I and James I, although the mason John Thorpe, who probably acted as Lord Dorset's surveyor, may also have had a hand in the design.

The pairs of caryatids on both levels and the panels of elaborate grotesque ornament are based largely on German and Flemish pattern-books, such as those of Wendel Dietterlin and Maarten de Vos. Almost barbaric in its vigour and the density of its decoration, the screen may originally have been painted, like the great achievement of the Sackville arms in the centre of the cresting. The dark shellac finish was applied in the Victorian period.

CEILING

The ceiling, with its geometric pattern of squares and circles, and the deep arcaded frieze are by Richard Dungan, James I's master plasterer, who was paid large amounts for plaster of Paris and 'fretts' at Knole in 1607–8.

The 1st Duke of Dorset returning to Dover Castle after taking the oath as Lord Warden of the Cinque Ports; by John Wootton, 1727/8 (no. 2; Great Hall)

(Left) The Great Hall

FIREPLACE

The fireplace was installed by the 1st Earl, though the original Jacobean chimneypiece and overmantel, with coupled columns and strapwork decoration in the same style as the screen, were removed in the late 18th century.

The polished steel and brass firedogs, which bear the arms and initials of Henry VIII and Anne Boleyn, were almost certainly made by Henry Romayne, the Royal locksmith, in 1533, and were bought before 1799 at a sale at Hever Castle, the former home of the Boleyns.

FLANKING CHIMNEYPIECE:

Pewter processional lights, acquired by the 1st Duke of Dorset. The electric uplighters were installed around 1900.

STAINED GLASS

IN WINDOW LEFT OF CHIMNEYPIECE:

The arms of Robert Devereux, 2nd Earl of Essex, a favourite of Queen Elizabeth.

IN OPPOSITE WALL, LEFT TO RIGHT:

The arms of Queen Elizabeth, Sackville, Sackville and de Vere.

PICTURES

(A separate handlist is available describing all the pictures on show at Knole.)

OVER CHIMNEYPIECE:

2 *The 1st Duke of Dorset returning to Dover Castle after taking the oath as Lord Warden of the Cinque Ports*
JOHN WOOTTON (1682–1764)
Painted immediately after the 1st Duke was appointed Lord Warden for the third time, on 4 January 1727/8. The splendid contemporary frame, in the style of William Kent, is decorated with the Sackville leopards and *vair* (stylised heraldic representation of squirrel skins).

FAR END, ON PANELLING:

1 *Thomas Sackville, 1st Earl of Dorset* (1536–1608)
Attributed to JOHN DE CRITZ (*c.*1552/3–1641/2)
The first Sackville owner of Knole, and the man who commissioned the decoration of this room and of the Great Staircase (see p. 61). It is characteristic that he should have had himself painted by the Serjeant-Painter to the King.

OVER DOOR TO GREAT STAIRCASE:

3 *Edward, 4th Earl of Dorset* (?1589–1652)
Studio of Sir ANTHONY VAN DYCK (1599–1641)
The key attached to the frame is said to be his key of office as Lord Chamberlain to Charles I.

THE GREAT STAIRCASE

Like the Great Hall, the staircase was entirely remodelled by Thomas, 1st Earl of Dorset, between 1605 and 1608. It formed a key stage in the formal procession of the family and their guests from the Great Hall to the state rooms on the first floor. The architectural scheme was influenced by the Renaissance revival of the classical orders, which are arranged in the correct sequence: Doric at the bottom, Ionic in the middle, Corinthian at the top.

DOOR-STOP

The mammoth door-stop in the form of Shakespeare came from Vita Sackville-West's bedroom. Her mother had a passion for fresh air, and insisted that all the doors were kept open.

SCULPTURE

IN LOBBY AT FOOT OF STAIRS:

A nude plaster figure of Giovanna Baccelli (d.1801), a celebrated dancer and the mistress of the 3rd Duke of Dorset, who acquired it in 1778, the year before she came to live at Knole (see p. 82). It is attributed to John Baptist Locatelli (*c.*1735–1805).

PICTURE

Gainsborough painting Giovanna Baccelli
BRITISH SCHOOL, *c.*1830–40
A romanticised image of Gainsborough painting his famous portrait (sold in 1890 and now in the Tate Gallery). Madame Baccelli is seen posing on a dais, while Wang-y-Tong, the Chinese pageboy painted by Reynolds (in the Reynolds Room), is seen coming in through a doorway. An engraving of Gainsborough's portrait stands nearby.

PAINTED DECORATION

'The Ascent of Man'

The 1st Earl was a poet and scholar who wanted his new staircase not just to provide a grand passageway, but also to describe a spiritual ascent. This is

The Great Staircase

reflected in the grisaille painted decoration, which illustrates how we can become better people in the journey through life.

The stages of human existence are represented by *The Four Ages of Man* under the lower arcade. These paintings are derived from engravings by Crispijn de Passe the Elder after Maarten de Vos published in 1596.

As we climb the stairs, we encounter paintings of *The Five Senses* after prints by Pieter de Iode: wisdom is to be gained not just from books, but also from using our senses – that is, by learning from experience. They depict, clockwise: *Smell* (flowers and dogs); *Taste* (ape and cornucopia of fruit); *Sight* (eagle and mirror); *Hearing* (viola da gamba and stag); *Touch* (tortoise and bird).

Once equipped with this experience, one will better appreciate the value of the social virtues, represented by the paintings around the upper landing: *The Triumph of Peace over War* and *Justice over Evil*, and other Virtues conquering Vices. These are again based on prints, by Johannes Sadeler I after Maarten de Vos, published in 1579, and by Crispijn de Passe.

Ornament

The figurative scenes on the stairs are surrounded by lavish cartouches and strapwork freely adapted from Jacob Floris's *Veelderhande cierlijke Comperte-menten ...* (1564). Between them are the Sackville leopards in *trompe l'oeil* echoing the magnificent leopards holding coats of arms on the newel posts of the staircase. Under the Virtues on the top landing are grotesques, adapted from a design by Cornelis Floris, published by Hieronymus Cock in 1554.

Most of the scheme was painted by Paul Isaacson. A master of the Painter Stainers Company in 1627, he is likely to have been the Paul 'Jackson' who painted the hall screen at Greenwich Palace for Queen Elizabeth in 1594, and who later worked for James I. Some of the painted decoration on the window wall at the base of the stairs is 18th-century, differing from the rest in its fluid rococo style and in the sophisticated painting of the leopards. The paintings were heavily restored in the early 20th century.

CEILING

The plasterwork ceiling has another geometrical design, this time of interlocking circles and quatrefoils, probably also the work of the King's plasterer, Richard Dungan.

LIGHTING

ABOVE WELL OF STAIRS:

The lantern, with a ratchet mechanism for raising and lowering it, is probably early 18th-century and original to the room, having been converted to gas and then electricity.

STAINED GLASS

The small heraldic quarries in the otherwise clear glass windows are mostly contemporary, showing the arms, crest and Garter of the 1st Earl of Dorset.

THE FIRST-FLOOR APARTMENTS

The staircase leads to the series of state rooms on the first floor known at least since the 18th century as the show rooms. These are arranged on a fairly consistent pattern of self-contained 'apartments', each consisting of a bedchamber, with a dressing-room or closet approached by a long gallery. There are three of these apartments, described here in the order in which they are now shown to visitors. They comprise:

The Brown Gallery, Spangle Bedroom and Dressing Room

The Leicester Gallery, Venetian Ambassador's Room and Dressing Room (now Museum Room)

The Cartoon Gallery, King's Room and Closet

THE BROWN GALLERY

This is part of Archbishop Bourchier's original mid-15th-century building, though remodelled by the 1st Earl of Dorset in the early 17th century. The 1st Earl probably used it as the withdrawing-room to the Spangle Bedroom at the far end on the left, as both have the same pattern of ceiling.

Long galleries of this kind not only acted as a communicating corridor, but also provided a place to take gentle exercise in bad weather and became a favourite setting for displaying portraits (see below).

DECORATION

The oak panelling and the ribbed ceiling, 88 feet in length, are of characteristic Jacobean design, though the pilasters may have been added later in the 17th century.

PICTURES

The rows of 16th- and early 17th-century portraits, hung on the long south wall, form a survey of famous figures from English, French and Netherlandish history of that period. This is, with Hardwick Hall in Derbyshire, the earliest surviving example of a portrait gallery in Britain. The original set of pictures comprises no fewer than six portraits of members of the Howard family, five prelates of the Church of England and leading – mostly Catholic – political figures from the Wars of Religion in France and the Netherlands. It may have been commissioned in the late 16th century by Lady Margaret Howard (d.1591), the wife of the 2nd Earl of Dorset, who himself seems to have added to the series portraits with a Protestant bias. The portraits of British sovereigns are by other artists and were added in the late 18th century, when most of the pictures were given matching 'ribbon' frames and inscriptions on scrolls.

FURNITURE

The Brown Gallery contains the first instalment of that unique collection of early English furniture for which Knole is particularly renowned. Most of the pieces were acquired by the 6th Earl of Dorset as perks or 'perquisites' during his time as Lord Chamberlain of the Household to William III, between 1689 and 1697. It was the Chamberlain's right to take for himself any of the furnishings in the royal palaces deemed to be worn out, or in any way outdated. In this way Lord Dorset brought to Knole a whole range of 17th-century royal furniture, dating in some cases back to the time of James I and Charles I. So much of their painted decoration and upholstery have survived, because large parts of Knole were used only intermittently over the following 200 years, and these pieces remained for long periods under dustsheets.

Of particular interest are:

AT ENTRANCE TO BROWN GALLERY:

A pair of superbly carved walnut chairs upholstered in blue silk damask in the style of Thomas Roberts, with their feet in the shape of dolphins, and the Royal Crown carved in their front stretchers. These bear the mark 'WP' beneath a crown (for Whitehall Palace) under their seats, and were evidently made for Charles II or James II.

LEFT OF THE ABOVE:

An armchair with a high shaped back and a pair of putti holding a crown on the front stretcher, made about 1685.

MIDDLE OF ROOM:

The X-framed armchairs are the most important of the early 17th-century furniture here. They derive from the Roman *sella curulis* (folding chairs often used on military campaigns) and are known in medieval inventories as 'Chairs of State', since they were used as thrones, placed on a dais below a canopy, and almost invariably flanked by two stools, with a lower footstool in front. Only one complete set now survives at Knole, that covered in purple velvet, appliqué with embroidery in silver, but many of the other chairs can be seen with their attendant stools.

The Brown Gallery

ON WINDOW SILL TO LEFT UNDER RED COVER:

Lacquer tray with porcelain flowers.

OPPOSITE LADY BETTY GERMAIN'S CHINA CLOSET:

An armchair, with a frame painted in a delicate arabesque pattern in white on a scarlet ground, probably intended to repeat the pattern of its original upholstery (later replaced by green velvet with silver fringe).

LEFT OF THE ABOVE:

An armchair entirely covered in silver brocade on a white background, with a floral design of an eastern Mediterranean type. The original, early 17th-century textile covering the legs is Italian, while the later 17th-century replacement on the seat back is French.

AT FAR END OF BROWN GALLERY:

An outsize cabriole armchair of the early 18th century, perhaps used by the 1st Duke on one of his embassies to Ireland, flanked by stools.

At the far end of the Brown Gallery, turn right into Lady Betty Germain's Rooms.

Lady Betty Germain, who lived in these rooms in the early 18th century; by Charles Philips, 1731 (no. 130; Lady Betty Germain's Sitting Room)

LADY BETTY GERMAIN'S ROOMS

These two small rooms are named after Lady Elizabeth Germain (1680–1769), who occupied them in the early 18th century during the lifetime of the 1st Duke of Dorset.

It is easy to picture Lady Betty stitching at the bed-curtains now hanging round her little four-poster; making pot-pourri, which is still made from her own recipe at Knole; chatting with the Dorsets and their children; writing many letters, some of them to Jonathan Swift, who had been her father's chaplain and whose portrait hangs in her sitting-room; and looking from her windows over the formal 17th-century garden to the trees of the park beyond. An agreeable existence, but perhaps not a very exciting one.

A daughter of the 2nd Earl of Berkeley and a distant relation of the Sackvilles, Lady Betty married Sir John Germain, from whom she inherited the great Mordaunt house of Drayton in Northamptonshire. Germain was a friend of the Duchess of Dorset's father, and is thought by some to have been William III's illegitimate half-brother. Lady Betty's close friendship with the 1st Duke and Duchess of Dorset led her, on her death in 1769, to leave Drayton to their youngest son, Lord George Sackville, who took the name of Germain and founded a branch of the Sackville family there (see p. 78).

LADY BETTY'S BEDROOM

DECORATION

The oak panelling, cornices and overmantels, which are decorated with grotesque ornament, are Jacobean, and were put up either by the 1st Earl in 1605–8 or by the 4th Earl, after he succeeded in 1624, to repair damage inflicted by a fire the previous year. Breaks in the beautifully carved decorative frieze suggest that it was imported from another room or house.

BED

The bed-hangings have canvas appliqués embroidered with floral designs in *gros point* using coloured wool. The headcloth and inner valances come from a late 17th-century or early 18th-century quilted bedset made of cream silk interlined with wool. The coverlet is of green silk embroidered with coloured wools in long and shot, satin and stem stitches, with French knots and couched cord outlines. The fringes and braids appear to be original.

OTHER FURNITURE

The set of six tall-backed armchairs of the William III period is unusual in being part-ebonised and part-silvered. Their seat covers have been made up from fragments of 17th-century Flemish tapestry.

The fire-screen has a base adapted from a 17th-century candlestand, surmounted by a Rococo frame, of about a hundred years later, possibly designed as the cresting for a mirror.

ON HEARTH:

The two simple iron cylinders pierced with holes are early candle-screens known as 'hundred-eye lanterns'. Candles that were used to light the rooms at night were stood in them to prevent accidents; the pattern that was thrown on the walls and ceiling gave rise to the name.

TAPESTRIES

Mid-17th-century Flemish verdure tapestries.

CARPET

The carpet is an extremely rare early 17th-century example of English turkey-work, and one of the most important textiles in the house.

Lady Betty Germain's Bedroom

LADY BETTY'S SITTING ROOM

PICTURES

LEFT OF DOOR:

130 *Lady Betty Germain* (1680–1769), 1731
CHARLES PHILIPS (1708–47)

The walls are crowded with small, mostly 17th-century, 'cabinet' pictures of the kind that were hung in small rooms like this from the 17th century. Many were bought by the 3rd Duke of Dorset on the Grand Tour in the 1770s from the dealers James Byres and Thomas Jenkins.

FURNITURE

FLANKING MIRROR:

A pair of walnut candlestands with brass mounts, in the style of Gerrit Jensen (active *c.*1680–1715), William III's cabinetmaker.

RIGHT OF CHIMNEYPIECE:

A pair of grained Restoration armchairs with stylised backs in the form of rows of balusters. The seat covers are of red silk decorated with applied silk motifs of a harp and a crown, which originally formed part of a large late 17th- or early 18th-century royal coat of arms.

Four walnut stools with cabriole legs. The seat covers are of crimson silk decorated with applied red and blue silk and embroidered with the royal arms of William and Mary and Queen Anne in gold and silver thread. The embroidery may have been adapted from tabards ordered by the Master of the Wardrobe for the state trumpeters.

FLANKING FIREPLACE:

A pair of dummy-board figures, representing a lady and gentleman dressed in the costume of the first decade of the 18th century. They were used as fire-screens or simply placed around the room – 'silent companions', as Vita Sackville-West evocatively described them.

A walnut spinning-wheel, probably late 18th-century.

MISCELLANEA

A fine piece of stumpwork, *c.*1650–80, representing *The Judgement of Paris.*

RIGHT OF WINDOW:

A frame of late 18th-century plaster intaglios cast from classical engraved gemstones, which were typical souvenirs of the Grand Tour in the 18th century.

THE SPANGLE BEDROOM

This is one of a series of rooms along the east front overlooking the garden, which were entirely rebuilt either by the 1st Earl of Dorset in 1605–8 or by the 4th Earl after the 1623 fire. The fact that the ground floor below is of medieval stone construction favours the fire damage theory, but the panelling of the rooms and the exterior of the façade, half-timbered and rendered, with eight identical gables and pedimented oriel windows, could well be of the 1st Earl's period on stylistic grounds.

DECORATION

The Jacobean panelling here is some of the finest in the house. The caryatids in the overmantel, and the delicate strapwork patterns used in the frieze and the pilasters flanking the two bay windows, are lighter and more refined than the carving on the Great Hall screen, though equally dependent on late 16th-century Netherlandish and French pattern-books. They were probably put up by the 1st Earl in 1605–8.

TAPESTRIES

The Brussels tapestries were woven in the second half of the 17th century by Hendrik Reydams, who signed them with his initials. They represent the stories of Cephalus and Procris and Mercury and Argus, both taken from Ovid's *Metamorphoses* – and are very probably therefore the '6 peces of Tapestry storys out of Ovid' taken by the 6th Earl from the ante-chamber of the Queen's apartments at White-hall in 1695, a few months after her death. They are hung here in typically casual 17th-century fashion covering the doors to prevent draughts.

BED

The magnificent bed is hung with crimson satin panels, decorated with an extremely rare appliqué strapwork pattern and originally sewn with small silver spangles or sequins, many of which remain, appearing, in their present, tarnished condition as black dots: it is these which have given the room its

The Spangle Bedroom

name. When new, the whole bed must have glittered as the breeze from the open window stirred the hangings.

The appliqué panels are of outstanding quality and may originally have formed part of a late 16th- or early 17th-century Canopy of State in a royal palace. It is possible that the 6th Earl's grandfather, Lionel Cranfield, acquired the panels in the early 17th century and had the curtains, with their Italian silk lining, made to match for Copt Hall in Essex. The 6th Earl may have applied both to the present bed framework, when the material came from Copt Hall to Knole in 1701. The bed was installed in its present position by 1765.

OTHER FURNITURE

The suite of furniture, consisting of an X-framed 'Chair of State' and eight other high stools, is covered with the same appliqué strapwork textile as the earlier parts of the bed.

AGAINST SOUTH WALL (OPPOSITE FIREPLACE):

The black and gold lacquer table, candlestands and pier-glass are attributed to William III's cabinetmaker, Gerrit Jensen, who charged the 6th Earl £18 for 'a Table, Stands and Glass Japan' in December 1690. The stamped brass borders round the tops of the candlestands and table are a rare feature, also associated with Jensen's other known work. The mirror unfortunately lacks its cresting, which may have been similarly ornamented.

METALWORK

ON TABLE, LEFT OF BED:

The toilet service, of filigree Indian, or Persian, silver, was probably acquired in the early 19th century by Lord Amherst, who married the 3rd Duke's daughter, Lady Mary Sackville.

The crimson silk hangings of the bed in the Spangle Bedroom have a Turkish-inspired appliqué strapwork pattern decorated with the silver sequins (now tarnished) from which the room takes its name

IN FIREPLACE:

A pair of magnificent late 17th-century brass andirons with urn-shaped finials.

CARPET

IN CENTRE OF ROOM:

A rare late 16th- or early 17th-century Mughal carpet with a dark red figured ground, probably acquired by the 6th Earl as a royal perk.

THE SPANGLE DRESSING ROOM

This room is so called because it served the adjoining bedchamber with its remarkable 'spangled' bed-hangings.

DECORATION

The oak panelling here is of the same pattern as that in the Leicester Gallery, but the chimneypiece and overmantel are more ornate even than those in the Spangle Bedroom.

FIREPLACE

The surround is of stone with a rectangular panel above it carved with scrolling acanthus. This in turn is framed by carved wooden Doric pilasters, which support Corinthian pilasters, again highly ornamented with strapwork. In the centre of the overmantel are the Sackville arms in a cartouche, and in the frieze above the pilasters is carved a pair of squatting demons with hoofed feet.

FURNITURE

The oak harpsichord case, though it has long since lost its mechanism, is of great importance, since it is signed above the keyboard by the London maker John Hasard or Haward, and dated 1622. This makes it the second earliest documented example of an English harpsichord, and suggests that it was bought either by the 3rd Earl and his wife, Lady Anne Clifford, or by Lionel Cranfield for Copt Hall.

The set of two walnut armchairs and six stools, covered in crimson silk damask, is of about 1670 and came from Whitehall Palace, two of the stools bearing a crown and the initials 'WP' stamped on the webbing under the seats. The front stretchers are particularly well carved, each with a basket of flowers set in acanthus.

MIDDLE OF ROOM:

The walnut side-table, of about 1690, is decorated with so-called 'oyster' veneers and with floral marquetry panels on the top.

The pair of Charles II footstools has legs and stretchers formed of scrolls, with tops covered with crimson silk damask, which may be late 17th-century.

The dummy-board figure of a young woman seated, peeling an apple, is probably Dutch of about 1700, and is painted over a tapestry-covered base.

PICTURES

The room was originally hung with tapestries, but by the end of the 18th century it held a dense mixture of subject pictures and portraits; three of the latter are still in it. Most of the portraits here now are of ladies at the Court of Charles II, painted by or after the leading Court artist Sir Peter Lely.

THE BILLIARD ROOM

Little more than a deep recess on the east side of the Leicester Gallery, the Billiard Room contains the original 17th-century billiard-table.

BILLIARD-TABLE

The ivory-tipped cues, known as 'maces' in the 17th and 18th centuries, are similar to those shown in use in an early 18th-century engraving depicting billiard-players, displayed on an easel near the table. At this time, players pushed the ball with the curved mace, rather than striking it. Straight cues did not become common until around 1800.

OTHER FURNITURE

RANGED ALONG TWO WALLS:

The set of nine Italian walnut chairs is of a type often known as 'campaign chairs' in the 17th century, since they are hinged and could be folded flat for use on military campaigns.

'DUMB BELL'

The rope suspended through a hole in the ceiling near the door to the Spangle Dressing Room was originally attached to an early 17th-century 'dumb bell' – a machine looking rather like·a windlass, carefully balanced with large lead weights on the ends of iron bars in the attic above. This provided the same exercise as pulling a bell rope in a church tower, but without causing any noise. The modern dumb-bell used for exercise takes its name from the shape of the weighted bars of such machines.

PICTURE

Of particular interest is:

ON FAR WALL, BESIDE ARCH INTO LEICESTER GALLERY:

167 *Thomas Durfey, writer of comedies and songs, and librarian at Knole* (1653–1723)
JOHN VAN DER GUCHT
Poet, composer and intimate of both Charles II and the 6th Earl, who gave him lodging at Knole for many years. He holds a book entitled *The Kingdom of the Birds*, probably in reference to his comic opera *Wonders in the Sun*, which gave an imaginary impression of bird life. Music and literature have been the passion of many generations of Sackvilles: the 1st Earl kept a private orchestra in the house,

and the 2nd Duke was one of the principal promoters of Italian opera in London in the early 18th century.

CERAMICS

IN CORNER LEFT OF WINDOW:

A three-part north Italian pottery vessel, bearing the arms of Pope Clement XI, *c.*1700–20. It was used as a stove.

A door to the left of the window leads to the Museum Room.

THE MUSEUM ROOM
(THE VENETIAN AMBASSADOR'S DRESSING ROOM)

This room was originally the dressing-room for the Venetian Ambassador's Room, with which it formed one of the three major apartments at Knole. It has since been adapted to provide ideal atmospheric conditions for some of the rarest and most fragile of the Knole textiles. Whatever precautions are taken, the textiles in the show rooms will eventually decay, but it is hoped that the life of those preserved in the Museum Room, where dust can be excluded and light, temperature and humidity controlled, will be prolonged indefinitely. In this way, a sample of Knole's unique inheritance of early textiles will be preserved for posterity.

FURNITURE

A settee and pair of stools covered in an early 18th-century silk with a design carried out in silver thread. Materials of this type, woven with exotic, elongated, swaying designs, are known as 'bizarre' silks. They were woven in Europe, notably at Lyons and at Spitalfields in London, mainly for dress material.

An armchair, dating from the 1680s, upholstered with a piece of fabric that has never seen daylight: its claret and emerald swirls give a vivid glimpse of Knole in its heyday.

An X-framed 'Chair of State', covered in a tissue of silver gilt, red and yellow with a red silk and silver-gilt fringe. It bears the Hampton Court stamp and date 1661.

The Knole settee

The 'Knole settee' is probably the most celebrated single piece of furniture in the house. The prototype of innumerable reproductions made from the late 19th century onwards, this distant ancestor of the modern sofa was originally used in a quite different, and more formal, context: placed beneath a canopy, like a 'Chair of State', in the state dressing-room or 'cabinet' beyond the bedchamber, it would have been used by the King or Queen (more likely the latter) when receiving the few honoured guests allowed to penetrate this inner sanctum. The couch was probably made just after the Restoration of 1660. In the Royal Warrants for 1660–1, the upholsterer John Casbert was paid for 'a large Couch of green damaske … [with] iron worke double gilt used about the Couche' – evidently a mechanism similar to the curious ratchets by which the cushioned side panels can be raised or lowered on the Knole settee. The red velvet and heavy brass nailing appear to be original.

PORCELAIN

Much of the porcelain in the display cabinet is French – Sèvres and Vincennes – and was acquired by the 3rd Duke, either on his first visit to Paris in 1769 or when he returned as ambassador in 1783–9. Of particular interest are:

ON LEFT-HAND SIDE OF DISPLAY CABINET:

A Sèvres tea service.

A ewer and basin and matching broth bowl; the former is painted with a pink spoonbill after Buffon, dated 1780.

CENTRE:

An early 19th-century Worcester service, bearing the crest of the Earl of Plymouth, first husband of the 3rd Duke's daughter, Mary (see p. 86).

RIGHT:

A Worcester service of 1750–75.

Cross the Leicester Gallery to the Venetian Ambassador's Room.

(Right) The Venetian Ambassador's Room

THE VENETIAN AMBASSADOR'S ROOM

'Green and gold ... of all rooms I never saw a room that so had over it a bloom like the bloom on a bowl of grapes and figs ... greens and pinks originally bright, now dusted and tarnished over.' Vita Sackville-West's evocative description of the faded magnificence of this room was echoed by Virginia Woolf in *Orlando*: 'The room ... shone like a shell that has lain at the bottom of the sea for centuries and has been crusted over and painted a million tints by the water; it was rose and yellow, green and sand-coloured. It was frail as a shell, as iridescent and as empty.'

The room derives its name from Nicolò Molino, Venetian ambassador to the Court of James I, whose full-length portrait by Mytens hangs to the right of the entrance in the Leicester Gallery, and who is said to have occupied it on a visit to Knole around 1622. Nothing of its Jacobean decoration survives, however, perhaps because of the fire which destroyed much of this end of the house in 1623.

DECORATION

The present decoration, which appropriately includes a Venetian window, with finely carved Ionic capitals and Palladian mouldings, was introduced by the 1st Duke about 1730. The Duke's architect is unknown, but the pedimented overmantel and the carved wood frieze are in the manner of William Kent, who may also have had a hand in remodelling Dorset House, in Whitehall, for the 1st Duke after 1725.

BED

State Bed with arms of James II, with two matching armchairs and six stools. The richly carved and gilded bed, with hangings of blue-green Genoa velvet,

and its suite of armchairs and stools were made for James II in 1688, and form one of the most splendid and historically important sets of late Stuart furniture in existence. The carving – including the King's monogram, the royal crown and lion and unicorn on the tester of the bed, and the chair frames supported by four draped figures, with trumpeting putti on the stretchers between – was almost certainly executed by Thomas Roberts. A royal warrant, dated August 1688, required the Master of the Wardrobe to supply 'a bed of green and gold figured velvet [now faded to a rust colour] with scarlet and white silk fringe', two armchairs and six stools for Whitehall. In November 1688, Roberts was paid for the same number of chairs and stools 'richly carved with figures and gilt all over with gold'.

Nicolò Molino, Venetian ambassador to the Court of James I. He is said to have occupied the room that now bears his name around 1622; by Daniel Mytens (no. 174; Leicester Gallery)

It is quite possible that this was the bed from which James II arose, only a month later, on the morning of 18 December 1688, to find Whitehall Palace surrounded by Dutch troops. The King then slipped away down the Thames on the royal barge to Rochester, from where he fled to France to spend the rest of his life in exile. It is hardly surprising, in view of these revolutionary events, that the subsequent Wardrobe accounts, which might have revealed the name of the upholsterer, were never made up. The Huguenot Jean Poitevin is perhaps the most likely candidate, since he received most of the other large commissions of this sort during James II's brief reign. The bed was, at any rate, brought to Copt Hall from Whitehall in 1695 as one of the 6th Earl's 'perquisites' after Queen Mary's death. It arrived at Knole six years later.

The strong smell is caused by the old wigs with which the mattress was found to be stuffed, when the bed was restored in the 1950s.

TAPESTRIES

The tapestry to the left of the bed depicts scenes from *Amadis de Gaule*, a romance of chivalry which became popular after a French translation was published in 1540. It was woven by François Spiering (1549/51–1631), whose Latinised signature appears in the bottom centre, probably in Delft *c*.1600. The other two tapestries come from a different series. Still in a remarkable state of preservation, they seem to have formed part of a large consignment of tapestries acquired by the 6th Earl from Whitehall Palace in 1695.

CARPET

The rare carpet is Indian, made in the early 17th century and close in design to contemporary Persian carpets.

THE LEICESTER GALLERY

This is named after the Earl of Leicester, to whom Queen Elizabeth granted Knole between 1561 and 1566, before its acquisition by Thomas Sackville.

DECORATION

The oak panelling with its frieze of strapwork cartouches, interspersed with brackets, and the fluted pilasters supporting the arch between the

The Leicester Gallery

Gallery and Billiard Room, are part of Thomas Sackville's work between 1605 and 1608.

ON RIGHT-HAND WALL:

The stone chimneypiece dates from Archbishop Bourchier's period in the 15th century.

FURNITURE

The principal interest of the Leicester Gallery lies in the remarkable collection of early 17th-century furniture, part of which was acquired from the royal palaces by the 6th Earl, either in his own capacity as Lord Chamberlain to William III, or through his maternal grandfather, Sir Lionel Cranfield (later 1st Earl of Middlesex), who held the post of Master of the Great Wardrobe in James I's reign.

RIGHT OF NEAR WINDOW:

Two 'Armada' chests, with elaborate locks, probably made in Nuremberg in the 17th century. They are decorated with flowers on a green ground.

The bottles were made on the estate and are stamped with the Sackville arms.

LEFT OF DOOR TO VENETIAN AMBASSADOR'S ROOM:

A set of four mid-17th-century elbow chairs with legs and arms of octagonal section, entirely upholstered in their original crimson silk damask, studded with brass nails. The width and architectural proportions of chairs like these were based on French fashions of the 1640s.

FLANKING CHIMNEYPIECE:

A pair of 17th-century Venetian candlestands, finely carved in the form of Nubian figures – a triton and a mermaid supporting gilded shells. These were

In Mytens's portrait of James I, the King sits on a chair of state very similar to that below it in the Leicester Gallery

probably among the 6th Earl's own acquisitions for Copt Hall, and brought to Knole in 1701.

FACING CHIMNEYPIECE:

A set of beechwood settees, chairs and stools, upholstered in their original red velvet and probably *c*.1625. Their frames are decorated with a gilded ground and an overlay of red glaze. Royal warrants of this date refer to similar sets 'paynted and guilte by John de Creete the Serjeante Paynter', and it is not inconceivable that de Critz (who collaborated with Inigo Jones on many of his masques) was himself responsible for this delicate design.

AT SOUTH END OF GALLERY, BENEATH PORTRAIT OF JAMES I:

An X-framed 'Chair of State', stamped on the webbing beneath the seat with the Hampton Court inventory mark and the date 1661; upholstered in red velvet, it is strikingly similar to the chair in which Mytens portrays the King. It dates either from the reign of James I or was made in a deliberately old-fashioned style in 1661, after the Restoration.

PICTURES

RIGHT OF DOOR TO VENETIAN AMBASSADOR'S ROOM:

174 *Nicolò Molino*, 1622
DANIEL MYTENS (*c*.1590–1647)
Venetian Ambassador to the Court of James I. Molino is holding a letter addressed to the King and bearing the seal of the Doge of Venice.

ON LEFT-HAND WALL, AT FAR END:

198 *Lady Martha Cranfield, Countess of Monmouth* (1601–67), *c*.1620
DANIEL MYTENS (*c*.1590–1647)
Her father, the 1st Earl of Middlesex, was one of Mytens's biggest patrons. Mytens was appointed Painter to King Charles I in 1625, and his sensitive – yet solemn – style is typical of Court portraits before the arrival of Van Dyck. Her sister married the 5th Earl of Dorset.

199 *A Gentleman with his Page*, 1642
WILLIAM DOBSON (*c*.1610/11–46)
This portrait probably depicts an officer in Charles I's service. Dobson painted the Royal Family and was described by his contemporary, John Aubrey, as 'the most excellent painter that England hath yet bred'.

196 *Lionel Cranfield, 1st Earl of Middlesex* (1575–1645)
DANIEL MYTENS (*c*.1590–1647)
His collections at Copt Hall came to Knole as a result of the marriage of his daughter, Frances, to the 5th Earl in 1637.

ON END WALL:

200 *James I* (1566–1625)
Studio of DANIEL MYTENS (*c*.1590–1647)
This version of Mytens's portrait, in a contemporary frame finely carved with putti and trailing acanthus branches, probably belonged to Lionel Cranfield. Note the similarity of the X-framed chair in the portrait to the chair below.

GLASSES

IN FRONT OF FIREPLACE:

The two long glasses are for 'a yard of ale'. They are traditionally known as 'My Lord's Conscience' and 'My Lady's Conscience', the latter being the longest.

LADY BETTY GERMAIN'S CHINA CLOSET

Following Queen Mary's passion for porcelain 'cabinets' – small rooms at Kensington and Hampton Court crammed with Delft and oriental blue-and-white – Lady Betty Germain amassed a considerable collection at her own house, Drayton in Northamptonshire, and is reputed to have owned some of the pieces still on the shelves of this small lobby. Most of the porcelain is Chinese, 18th-century; later additions include early Worcester.

ON LEFT-HAND SIDE:

Many of these mostly Chinese pieces are typical of the remains of services dating between 1720 and 1780.

IN CENTRAL CASE:

A Lambeth Delft posset pot, *c*.1780 (or 1700?) (bottom shelf, towards right). Posset was a kind of punch made with hot milk.

A Japanese blue-and-white ewer, *c*.1675 (top shelf, middle).

ON RIGHT-HAND SIDE:

A ginger jar, *c*.1640, which remained at Drayton until recently (top shelf, middle).

The large famille verte charger (bottom shelf, middle), painted in the centre with a Buddhistic lion playing with a brocaded ball, is typical of the finest large export pieces bought for houses such as Knole in the early 18th century.

The window overlooks the Water Court, with the great kitchen built by Archbishop Bourchier in the 15th century occupying the right-hand range. The name derives from the well which once stood here, and which must have served the kitchen. The rest of the buildings are mostly timber-framed and rendered in plaster, with overhanging windows and large gables – not unlike London merchants' houses of the early 17th century, and in direct contrast to the symmetrical stone façades of the two main courtyards.

The visitor now returns along the Brown Gallery, on the way to an entirely different part of the house. From the closet between the Gallery and the Ballroom a window looks out on to yet another small courtyard, timber-framed on all four sides, and probably of the 1st Earl's time. This has been known as the Pheasant Court since the mid-19th century. Lord Amherst, who had been Ambassador in China, brought back to England some of the species which now bear his name, and reared them here.

THE BALLROOM

The actual structure of this immense room is part of Archbishop Bourchier's work of about 1467, designed as the Solar, chief living-room or Great Chamber, to which the Archbishop and his attendants would have retired after eating at the high table in the Great Hall.

The present panelling and decoration were introduced by the 1st Earl between 1603 and his death in 1608. He would no doubt have dined here rather

The Ballroom

The mermaid frieze in the Ballroom

than in the Great Hall: in 1705 this was still called 'ye great Dining Roome'. The 1st Earl's accounts suggest that the craftsmen involved were again the King's carpenter and plasterer William Portington and Richard Dungan, with the addition of the mason Cornelius Cure, who is credited with the tomb of Mary, Queen of Scots in Westminster Abbey.

To imagine what the Great Chamber looked like then, you simply have to strip it in your mind's eye of all the existing furniture, and to furnish it sparsely with a few portraits and pieces of furniture, and some wall-hangings and tapestries for warmth and decoration. The elaborate screens, ceilings and friezes were all the decoration that would have been required to create the impression of grandeur that Thomas Sackville wished to convey.

DECORATION

William Portington was almost certainly responsible for the elaborate oak panelling with its repeated oval pattern (probably always painted ivory white, as it now is), the Composite pilasters beautifully decorated with strapwork (based on Vredeman de Vries's *Architectura* [1565]) and with winged horses springing out of their capitals. Above is the extraordinarily rich frieze, carved with pairs of mermaids, mermen and hippocamps (seahorses), separated by grotesque squatting figures.

CEILING

Richard Dungan's plasterwork ceiling is equally accomplished, its broad flat bands in a complex geometrical pattern complementing the panelling, and at the same time relieved by delicate bunches of flowers and foliage in the intervening spaces.

CHIMNEYPIECE

The great chimneypiece and overmantel rise the whole height of the room and rank among the finest works of Renaissance sculpture in England. In December 1607 the master mason to the Crown, Cornelius Cure, was paid £26 10s 'for stones for a chimney piece in the Wth drawing Chamber at Knoll'. The materials used are black, white and grey marbles and alabaster. The grey marble, quarried locally at Bethersden, near Ashford, is used to particularly beautiful effect in the broad lintel above the fireplace, incised so that the 1st Earl's arms and Garter, and the luxuriant acanthus scrolls either side, stand out polished against a matt background. Black marble provides the background for the exquisite alabaster garlands of flowers and musical instruments in the overmantel: a reminder that music would almost certainly have been performed in this room.

PICTURES

The room is now hung with full-length family portraits, many of them in their original 17th- and 18th-century frames.

ON WALL OPPOSITE FIREPLACE:

222 *Arabella Diana Cope, Duchess of Dorset* (1769–1825), 1803
ELISABETH VIGÉE-LEBRUN (1755–1842)
This portrait of the 3rd Duke's pretty young widow contrasts with the more formidable figure painted by John Hoppner thirteen years previously (no. 256; now hanging in the Reynolds Room).

223 *George John Frederick Sackville, 4th Duke of Dorset* (1793–1815)
GEORGE SANDARS (1774–1846)
This handsome young man was tragically killed in a riding accident in Ireland, at the age of 21.

LEFT OF BAY WINDOW:

227 *Charles Sackville, 6th Earl of Dorset* (1638–1706), 1694
Sir GODFREY KNELLER (1646/9–1723)
Described by his grandson as the 'Patron of Men of Genius and the Dupe of Women', the 6th Earl was a Restoration rake, who eventually brought to Knole most of the house's outstanding collection of furniture and textiles.

LEFT OF CHIMNEYPIECE:

233 *Richard Sackville, 3rd Earl of Dorset* (1589–1624), 1613
? WILLIAM LARKIN (1580s–1619)
Painted in 1613, the year of Dorset's spectacular appearance at the marriage of James I's daughter. His costume was so magnificent that the gossip John Chamberlain wrote '. . . It were long and tedious to tell you all the particularities of the excessive bravery both of men and women . . . but above all they speak of the Earl of Dorset.'

RIGHT OF CHIMNEYPIECE:

234 *Mary Curzon, Countess of Dorset* (d.1645), 1612
? WILLIAM LARKIN (1580s–1619)
Painted in 1612, the year of her marriage to Edward Sackville, younger brother of the 3rd Earl and himself later the 4th Earl. In 1630 Mary was appointed governess to Charles, Prince of Wales (later Charles II), and James, Duke of York (later James II). Costume pieces such as this are typical of Larkin; note how the portrait draws as much attention to the embroidered dress, the crimson underskirt decorated with pearls and silver fringing, and the rosettes in pink and blue around the neckline, as to the subject herself.

235 *Charles Sackville, later 2nd Duke of Dorset, as a Roman Consul* (1711–69)
FRANZ FERDINAND RICHTER
Commemorates a masque the 2nd Duke (then Lord Middlesex) staged in Florence in March 1737, while on the Grand Tour. He played a Roman consul returning on horseback to a Triumph.

ON WALL FACING WINDOW:

236 *Frances Cranfield, Countess of Dorset* (d.1687)
Sir ANTHONY VAN DYCK (1599–1641)
Frances Cranfield was the daughter of the 1st Earl of Middlesex, one of the wealthiest men in England; her marriage in 1637 to Richard, 5th Earl of Dorset helped to restore the fortunes of Knole in the second half of the 17th century.

237 *Lionel Sackville, later 7th Earl and 1st Duke of Dorset* (1687–1765), *and his sister, Mary, afterwards Duchess of Beaufort* (1687–1705), *as children*
Sir GODFREY KNELLER (1646/9–1723)

FURNITURE

The furniture, of all dates, is now arranged in 19th-century fashion in the centre of the room as well as against the walls. Some of the French pieces may have been collected by the 3rd Duke, who is known to have made many purchases from the *marchand-mercier*, or dealer, Dominique Daguerre, during his time as ambassador to Louis XVI from 1783 to 1789.

IN CENTRE OF ROOM:

The set of gilt armchairs and stools, carved with cherubs' heads at each corner, and swags of foliage, was either among the royal pieces acquired by the 6th Earl as Lord Chamberlain, or purchased by him from one of the French upholsterers that he patronised, such as Francis Lapiere.

IN CENTRE OF ROOM:

The Parisian carved and gilt day-bed is 17th-century and a rare surviving example.

IN CENTRE OF ROOM, IN FRONT OF FIREPLACE:

The late 17th-century fire-screen is similar to a documented example still in the Royal Collection by the Huguenot maker Jean Pelletier.

FLANKING CHIMNEYPIECE:

The pair of low Indian chairs, covered with silk, may be those described in the 1705 inventory as '2 Indian nurceing chairs'.

RIGHT OF CHIMNEYPIECE, ON TABLE:

The small ormolu clock, stamped by the *fondeur* J.-J. de Saint-Germain (1720–91), and with a mechanism by the Parisian clockmaker Alexis Huau, dates from the 1780s.

One of the wall-sconces, bearing the 1st Duke's coronet and Garter, about 1720, in the Ballroom

ON WALL OPPOSITE WINDOW:

An Italian cassone, or chest, inset with three mid-16th-century painted panels, representing a Roman triumph on the front, and Pompey and Marcus Curtius on the two sides. The note inside the lid is inscribed 'Florence 24th June 1876', which suggests that the *cassone* was acquired by the 1st Lord Sackville.

ON WALL FACING CHIMNEYPIECE:

The gilt table with a marble top, carved with a lion's mask in the apron, was probably acquired by the 1st Duke about 1720, together with the two series of splendid carved and gilt wall sconces above bearing his coronet and Garter, which are close in style to some of William Kent's designs. It is thought that these pieces were made for Dorset House in London, which Kent may have helped to decorate.

LEFT OF BAY WINDOW:

A Boulle table of ebony inlaid with brass and tortoiseshell, in the style of Levasseur, of the 1780s, when the 3rd Duke was in Paris.

ON PEDESTAL, RIGHT OF BAY WINDOW:

A Boulle clock, by Estienne Baillon.

RIGHT OF BAY WINDOW:

The Boulle writing-table with an inlaid top is of the late Louis XIV period (early 18th century), though it could well have been acquired by the 3rd Duke in Paris in the 1780s.

CARPET

The very large and rare carpet is 17th-century Indian, using a design similar to the rugs made at Herat.

THE SECOND PAINTED STAIRCASE

Between the Ballroom and the Reynolds Room, a small staircase, constructed in 1603–8, leads down to the private rooms, and upwards into the Retainers' Gallery and the attics, which occupy the top storey of the house.

DECORATION

The walls were painted in grisaille with trophies of weapons and the arms and cipher of the 1st Duke by Mark Antony Hauduroy. The artist, who was also responsible for decorating the King's Room, was paid for his work at Knole in 1723–4. He had earlier worked at Dyrham Park in Gloucestershire, where his father or brother, Samuel, designed the south front of the house.

THE REYNOLDS ROOM OR CRIMSON DRAWING ROOM

These alternative names derive from the fact that the walls are hung with a rare early 18th-century crimson stamped woollen velvet known as 'caffoy', and that most of the paintings shown against it are by Sir Joshua Reynolds. The room itself is much earlier in date: the stone doorcase on to the staircase has mid-15th-century mouldings, showing that this was part of Archbishop Bourchier's original building, though the plasterwork ceiling, the chimneypiece and the overmantel are all part of the 1st Earl's early Jacobean remodelling. In the 17th and 18th centuries, the room would have served as a withdrawing chamber, to which the family would have retired from the Great Chamber for private meals, and peace and quiet.

DECORATION

The plasterwork ceiling, by Richard Dungan, is not quite as elaborate as in the Ballroom; it incorporates the Sackville leopards, between broad interlacing ribs.

CHIMNEYPIECE

The chimneypiece is as splendid as its predecessor in the Ballroom. Caryatids in the Flemish fashion, with bronze heads and feet (probably intended to be gilded), flank the fireplace, while, above, putti holding huge trophies of arms ride on the backs of a pair of sphinxes. The pilasters on each side of the overmantel are again of Bethersden marble, incised to form the most delicate pattern of strawberries and wild flowers. The whole composition is based on French and Dutch engravings, including Du Cerceau's *Second Livre d'Architecture* (1561).

IN FIREPLACE:

The pair of silver andirons, with large finials in the shape of putti with a bellows and ash shovel standing on covered urns, bear the arms of Sackville and Cranfield on their bases, and were presumably made for the 5th Earl and his wife, Lady Frances Cranfield, *c.*1670.

PICTURES

ON FAR WALL, TOP LEFT:

249 *Wang-y-Tong, a Chinese Page at Knole*
Sir JOSHUA REYNOLDS, PRA (1723–92)
Sitting wistfully on a bamboo sofa, the square toes of his red shoes forming beautiful red highlights against the crimson and blue of his robes, Wang-y-Tong brings a touch of oriental exoticism to Knole. The Chinese page-boy was brought to England from Canton by John Bradby Blake, a contemporary of the 3rd Duke at Westminster School and an official of the East India Company. Wang-y-Tong obviously attracted the attention of the Duke, who took him into his service at Knole – where the English servants called him Warnoton – and had him educated at the grammar school in Sevenoaks.

BELOW WANG-Y-TONG:

261 *David Garrick* (1717–79)
Sir JOSHUA REYNOLDS, PRA (1723–92)
Garrick dominated the London theatre for 30 years during the second half of the 18th century, and was a close friend of Reynolds and Johnson. Painted in 1776, the year of his last appearance on stage, he is shown composing a prologue to be delivered at the start of a performance.

MIDDLE:

251 *Lord George, afterwards Viscount, Sackville* (1716–85)
THOMAS GAINSBOROUGH, RA (1727–88)
This large, authoritative man was one of the ablest members of his family and the one who came closest to achieving the highest office. He provoked immense controversy after being accused of disobeying orders at the Battle of Minden, and went on to become Secretary of State for the American Colonies at the time of their surrender.

BOTTOM RIGHT:

254 *Oliver Goldsmith* (1728–74), 1770
Sir JOSHUA REYNOLDS, PRA (1723–92)
The playwright and poet, whose works include *She Stoops to Conquer* and *The Vicar of Wakefield*, was a close friend of Reynolds and a founder member, with Reynolds and Dr Johnson, of the select 'Literary Club' established in 1765. The portrait was bought by the 3rd Duke.

The Reynolds Room

LEFT OF CHIMNEYPIECE:

255 *John Frederick Sackville, 3rd Duke of Dorset*
(1745–99), 1769
Sir JOSHUA REYNOLDS, PRA (1723–92)
The 3rd Duke, the only really serious picture col-
lector in the Sackville family, paid 150 guineas for
this full-length portrait in peer's robes.

RIGHT OF CHIMNEYPIECE:

256 *Arabella Diana Cope, Duchess of Dorset*
(1769–1825), 1790
JOHN HOPPNER (1758–1810)
Painted in the year she married the 3rd Duke.

NEAR WALL, BOTTOM LEFT:

250 *Sir Joshua Reynolds* (1723–92)
Sir JOSHUA REYNOLDS, PRA (1723–92)
Reynolds presented this self-portrait to the 3rd
Duke, a close friend and possibly his biggest patron,
in 1780.

TOP CENTRE:

259 *Ugolino and his Children in the Dungeon*, 1773
Sir JOSHUA REYNOLDS, PRA (1723–92)
This was Reynolds's most ambitious history painting, taking as its subject the gruesome tale of im-
prisonment, starvation and cannibalism found in
Dante's *Inferno*. Count Ugolino is incarcerated with
his two sons and two grandsons, when he realises
that the gaoler has no intention of bringing them
food. One by one, the children die, leaving the
Count with the stark decision of whether to starve
or to sustain his life through eating them. Reynolds

The 3rd Duke's Chinese page, Wang-y-Tong; by Sir Joshua Reynolds (no. 249; Reynolds Room)

paints the moment when Ugolino realises his fate, and his son Anselmo demands to know the reason for Ugolino's despair. When shown at the Royal Academy in 1773, it excited more discussion than any other British picture of its time. Two years later, the 3rd Duke paid the high price of 400 guineas for it.

BOTTOM RIGHT:

258 *Dr Samuel Johnson* (1709–84)
Sir JOSHUA REYNOLDS, PRA (1723–92)
Fanny Burney thought this portrait of the great dictionary-compiler and conversationalist, which the 3rd Duke bought in 1769, 'extremely like'.

CARPET

The Indian carpet belongs to a small but important group of so-called 'Portuguese' carpets, made in the Portuguese colony of Goa in the early 17th century. The small scenes in each of the four corners (look out for the sailors wearing Portuguese costumes and the European ships sailing towards the decorative border) are thought to represent the assassination of

Bahadur Shah, Sultan of Gujarat, while visiting the Portuguese fleet at Diu. Like the three other early Indian carpets at Knole, it may have been acquired from one of the royal palaces by the 6th Earl among his 'perquisites' as Lord Chamberlain after the death of Queen Mary II in 1694.

FURNITURE

AGAINST WALLS:

The walnut settees and chairs are of a simple early 18th-century form with cabriole legs, and make up part of a large set spread between this room and the Cartoon Gallery. Their particular interest lies in the original upholstery, which matches the hangings of the walls. It is a stamped woollen velvet or plush, frequently mentioned in 18th-century accounts, but now exceptionally rare. Some of the chairs also preserve their original knotted linen fringe.

BETWEEN WINDOWS:

The gilt pier-glass is another Kentian piece, acquired by the 1st Duke, whose arms are carved in the broken pediment.

THE CARTOON GALLERY

The Cartoon Gallery is the third of the long galleries at Knole that lead via withdrawing-rooms (in this case, the Reynolds Room) from the Great Chamber or Ballroom to the principal bedroom suites (in this case, the King's Room). The 17th-century lawyer and historian Roger North could have been describing the Cartoon Gallery when he wrote:

[the country-house gallery] ... should be easy of access, and for that reason it should be upon the first floor ... it must be laid in the most joyous, and diverting part of the house without any offence to the eye ... but all fronting the garden and viewing it from the best place. For this place, intended to entertain and divert the best company cannot be too much composed to that design ... And I think it is a great compliment to a gallery to have some breaks, in the nature of bow windows, not such as are Gothick ... but squares ... But these recesses are for select companies to converse in ... being as small with drawing rooms to the grand tour of the gallery ... I cannot but reiterate the recommendation of them, because they do not onely accomplish the gallery within, but are a beauty without.

Early inventories call the Cartoon Gallery the 'Matted Gallery' – perhaps because the vast Jacobean floorboards which are such a feature of the room were originally covered by rush matting, like that still found at Hardwick. The room now takes its name from a set of six large copies of Raphael's cartoons.

CARTOONS

FROM RIGHT TO LEFT:

Scenes from the Lives of SS. Peter and Paul, after the Tapestry Cartoons of Raphael

The Death of Ananias

The Blinding of Elymas

The Healing of the Lame Man at the Gate of the Temple

The Miraculous Draught of Fishes

Christ's Charge to St Peter

The Sacrifice at Lystra

A cartoon was originally a full-scale design for a tapestry or painting. The tapestries, for which the High Renaissance artist Raphael's original cartoons were designs, were commissioned by Pope Leo X in 1515–16 to hang in the Sistine Chapel in Rome, which was then regarded as the most splendid room in Christendom. The Pope chose the themes to reflect the dynamic history of the early church, the power of the Apostles, and the glory of the office of Pope. Originally, there were ten cartoons, of which seven survived. In 1623 Prince Charles, later Charles I, purchased these seven for £300, and they were then used as working drawings for the many sets of tapestries produced at the Mortlake Tapestry Factory. In 1624 the Flemish artist Franz Cleyn was brought to Mortlake to give expert guidance to the weavers, and it is then that he may have painted the six Knole copies (Knole is missing the seventh surviving cartoon, *St Paul preaching*). The Raphael cartoons themselves were lent by Prince Albert in 1865 to the Victoria & Albert Museum, where they

The Cartoon Gallery

remain. The Cleyn copies are said to have been presented by Charles I to the 1st Earl of Middlesex. They were kept at Copt Hall until 1701, when the house was sold by his grandson, the 6th Earl of Dorset, who brought them to Knole.

DECORATION

As in most other show rooms, the decoration of the gallery was carried out for the 1st Earl. The Corinthian pilasters framing the bay windows and the deep recess half way down the Gallery are also ornately carved with 'grotesques', including caryatid figures, birds, monkeys, garlands of fruit and flowers, and at the top of each a ram's mask – the old crest of the Sackvilles – with the leopard rampant in the frieze above the pilasters. In March 1608 the painter Paul Isaacson was paid £100 'for painting and guilding work in Yor lo: Gallery at Knoll', which must have included the naturalistic colours in which the pilasters are still picked out, and the *trompe-l'oeil* arabesque panels of the dado.

CEILING

The plasterwork ceiling by Richard Dungan differs from the others in having no square or intersecting panels, merely serpentine ribs which give a marvellous rippling effect of light and shade seen down the whole length of the Gallery. The spaces between the ribs are again filled by shallow reliefs of botanical emblems, probably taken by the plasterer from the woodcuts of some late 16th-century herbal.

CHIMNEYPIECE

Paired caryatids appear in the overmantel, another sumptuous composition of different varieties of marble and alabaster. The silver andirons, similar to those in the Reynolds Room, were made in the 1670s.

STAINED GLASS

Stained-glass shields record the alliances of the Sackville family from the 12th to the 17th centuries; these are older than the glass panels in the Great Hall, and may possibly have come from Buckhurst, the Sackvilles' house in Sussex. In the upper sections of two of the windows is a series of ten smaller armorial panels, representing lawyers and parliamentarians of the late 16th century, who were presumably among the friends of Sir Richard Sackville and his son, the 1st Earl.

PICTURES

ON NEAR WALL, JUST INSIDE DOOR FROM REYNOLDS ROOM:

285 *Henry Howard, Earl of Surrey* (c.1517–47)
Studio of GUILLIM SCROTS (active 1537–53)
Courtier and poet, who fell foul of Henry VIII in the last years of his reign. He was executed for high treason for joining the royal arms with his own. The 16th- or early 17th-century frame is particularly rare.

FURNITURE

ON NEAR WALL, JUST INSIDE DOOR FROM REYNOLDS ROOM:

The gilt table and pair of candlestands are thought to have been given by Louis XIV to the 6th Earl in 1670–1. Lord Buckhurst, as he then was, had been sent as ambassador to France to congratulate Louis on the successful completion of the secret Treaty of Dover, by which Charles II was to receive £200,000 a year from the French king in return for making war, jointly with Louis, against the Dutch. Look out for the fleur-de-lis, the armorial emblem of the kings of France, on each of the four bottom corners of the table frame – which support the furniture's royal French provenance. A payment made by the *Trésorier royal* at this date, apparently for these pieces, establishes that the frames were carved by Mathieu Lespagnandelle and gilded by David Dupré, and that the tops, inlaid with pewter and brass, were supplied by Pierre Gole, the principal supplier of furniture to Versailles in the 1670s and the founder of the Louis XIV style. From this account, there appear originally to have been two tables and four candlestands: the stands here represent only two of the Four Seasons, one carved with wheat for summer, the other with grapes for autumn.

ALONG RIGHT-HAND WALL:

Late 17th-century walnut armchairs and stools acquired by the 6th Earl from the royal palaces between 1689 and 1697. The finest of these (to the left of the chimneypiece) has its front stretcher carved with putti supporting the royal crown.

ALONG LEFT-HAND WALL:

Seven Charles II carved oak elbow chairs with cane backs.

(Right) A gilt mirror and pilasters, painted by Paul Isaacson about 1608, in the Cartoon Gallery

BETWEEN WINDOWS:

A pair of pier-glasses; their ebonised frames are inlaid with pierced gilt brass, chased with swirling acanthus patterns, and have retained their original 17th-century cresting.

FLANKING CHIMNEYPIECE:

17th-century Venetian candlestands in the form of blackamoors holding tambourines.

AT FAR END:

The remainder of the set of 'caffoy' chairs and settees, seen in the Reynolds Room.

AT FAR END, SET ACROSS BAY WINDOW
OVERLOOKING GREEN COURT:

A large 18th- or early 19th-century Chinese table, thought to have been brought back by Earl Amherst from his embassy to China in 1816 – with three large porcelain jars now placed on it.

The gilt table and candlestands in the Cartoon Gallery are thought to have been given to the 6th Earl by Louis XIV in 1670–71

AGAINST RIGHT-HAND WALL, TOWARDS FAR END
OF ROOM:

The large 'Russia' leather coffer or trunk, decorated with brass nails in elaborate patterns, has been attributed to Richard Pigg, coffer-maker to Charles II.

MUSICAL INSTRUMENTS

IN RECESS OPPOSITE CHIMNEYPIECE:

A Kirckman harpsichord.

A late 18th-century mahogany violin case painted with the monogram of the 3rd Duke. These are reminders that the musical traditions of Knole continued long after the 1st Earl's day.

METALWORK

ON DOORS:

The chased brass lock plates on the doors bear the monogram of William III, and were probably made by the locksmith Joseph Key. Another of the 6th Earl's 'perquisites', these may have been survivors of the disastrous fire which destroyed most of Whitehall Palace in 1698.

THE KING'S CLOSET

A door at the end of the Cartoon Gallery leads to the King's Room through a lobby flanked by two small closets. The closet on the left (not shown to visitors) would have been the 'dark closet' where the close stool, an elaborate chamberpot, was once kept. In France, such rooms were known as *lieux*

d'aisance (literally, places of easement), from which the English word 'loo' is derived.

The closet on the right, which would have been used as a dressing-room, is of interest for its rare late 17th-century wall-hangings – a rough-textured mohair, dyed green, watered (or moiré) and stamped to resemble silk damask, still bordered with its original woollen tasselled fringe. Material like this is described in early inventories, but practically no other examples of it survive.

FURNITURE

ON RIGHT, NEAR DOOR:

The close stool, upholstered in crimson velvet, is likely to have been acquired from Whitehall Palace by the 6th Earl. Given its grand appearance, it was almost certainly used as a 'royal seat of easement' by either of the two later Stuart kings, Charles II or James II,

The King's Closet

before being discarded during the reign of William III. The close stool would originally have had a pan or basin inside, probably made of pewter, with another as a replacement, for use while the first was being emptied.

ON RIGHT:

A pair of painted wooden candlestands, probably early 17th-century, are perhaps (with the long table in the Hall) among the very few pieces from the 1st Earl's period to have survived the plunder of Knole during the Commonwealth.

ON LEFT:

A small ebonised mirror is engraved with the 6th Earl's arms, and has an inscription in the cresting which records his installation as a Knight of the Garter in February 1691.

AT FAR END OF CLOSET:

A late 16th-century Italian walnut cassone, richly carved and gilded. The leopard badge of the Sackvilles has been painted on the centre of the oval cartouche on the front. You may have noticed the *cassone*'s companion, since painted black, in the outer gatehouse opposite the ticket office.

THE KING'S ROOM

The short flight of steps up to the King's Room, denoting a change in floor level, suggests that the tower which it occupies may have been an addition to Bourchier's mid-15th-century house, perhaps made by his successor Archbishop Morton between 1487 and 1500. The bay window was extended to the south still later, by the 1st Earl. Tradition has it that James I occupied the room on a visit to Knole soon afterwards – hence its present name.

Natural light, which tends to fade fabrics, is excluded from the room, and visitors view the works of art by electric light from within a glazed box. This provides more or less static atmospheric conditions and protects the sensitive fabrics in the room from dust. These measures also have the effect of bathing the room in the warm glow of candlelight, in which the gilding, the cloth of gold and the silver furniture smoulder in a perpetual evening light.

DECORATION

The fine plasterwork ceiling, presumed to be by Richard Dungan, dates from 1607–8 and formed part of the 1st Earl's remodelling of Knole.

The dado panelling and window reveals were painted in grisaille by Mark Antony Hauduroy for the 1st Duke in 1723–4.

TAPESTRIES

The tapestries hung all round the room above the dado are late 17th-century, made in London, and signed with the initials T.P. for Thomas Poyntz. They represent scenes from the story of the Babylonian king Nebuchadnezzar and are included in the list of goods brought to Knole from Copt Hall in 1701 by the 6th Earl.

FURNITURE

The contents of the King's Room provide a triumphant climax to the tour of Knole, as astonishing to 18th- and 19th-century tourists as they are to visitors today. Millais used the room as the setting for his celebrated picture, *The Eve of St Agnes*, painted in 1863, while a hundred years earlier Horace Walpole, Mrs Lybbe Powys and Fanny Burney all marvelled at the ebony cabinets and the silver furniture, and in particular the state bed with its matching chairs and stools, entirely covered with gold and silver brocade. Early guidebooks, recording James I's visit, assumed that the furniture was also Jacobean, but it is clear that the bed and its suite are late 17th-century and, like so many other pieces at Knole, were brought from Whitehall Palace by the 6th Earl, as part of his Lord Chamberlain's 'perquisites' after the death of Queen Mary in December 1694.

BED AND BED FURNITURE

The Royal State Bed was almost certainly made for James II, when still Duke of York, rather than for James I. The device on the headboard and chair frames is the coronet of a royal duke rather than the crown of the sovereign. Recent research suggests that the bed and its furniture are more likely to be French than English, perhaps supplied by Louis XIV's upholsterer Jean Peyrard, who paid visits to England in 1672 and 1673, bringing no fewer than six beds for Charles II. 1673 was also the year of James's marriage to Mary of Modena, and the chairs and stools at Knole, carved with little cupids hold-

The King's Room

ing bows and quivers, and billing doves, may have been intended to celebrate this event. Like many other objects at Knole, the bed was acquired as a perk by the 6th Earl.

The rare combination of gilding and silvering was found under a layer of black paint (that had probably been applied during a period of mourning) and was subsequently restored; the black paint can still be seen, however, on the finely carved feet of the bed, each with three crouching lions, and on the two low squab frames, listed in the 1705 inventory as having two cushions each, one to match the outside and one the inside of the bed.

Because of the effects of daylight and dust, and

the sheer weight of the gold and silver thread used, the bed-hangings had already begun to decay by the early 19th century, when Maria Edgeworth described 'in the silver room a bed, as the show woman trumpetted forth, of gold tissue which cost 8 thousand guineas new, now in tarnished tatters not worth Christies best puffing 8 thousand pence this day'. Conservation work began in 1974, painstakingly carried out at Knole by a team of up to 200 volunteers, who came in groups of 10–15 every day to work under expert guidance. Each of the six curtains alone involved an estimated 8,000–9,000 hours of work. Conservation was completed in 1987. Although the crimson and white of the ostrich plumes and the 'Cherry Coloured Satin' of the lining have long since flown (and only traces of it can be found in folds never exposed to daylight),

The King's Room in the mid-19th century, when the dressing table still had its original silk cover (or 'toylett') and the bed-curtains had their pink satin lining; by W. S. P. Henderson (private collection)

the King's Bed remains one of the great treasures of Knole, the most magnificent example of a state bed of the Louis XIV period to have survived anywhere in the world.

SILVER FURNITURE

Following the fashion set by Louis XIV, the 'Sun King', at Versailles, silver furniture was made in England after 1660 until about 1710. In France, every piece was melted down on the King's orders in 1689 and 1709 to pay for his military campaigns. Although a lot was also melted down in England, some survives, including the celebrated and rare silver furniture in the King's Room. It has been in this room since at least 1706 and its survival gives a good idea of the luxury that once adorned Knole and the royal palaces.

ON LEFT WALL:

The large four-handled salver, engraved with a hunting scene and the Sackville arms, is dated 1662.

LEFT OF WINDOW:

The silver table bears the London hallmark for 1680–1 and the monogram FCD, for Frances Cranfield, Countess of Dorset; a bill for this piece from the Anglo-Dutch cabinetmaker Gerrit Jensen, dated 1680, has recently been discovered. The oval plaque in the centre of the top represents the musical contest between Pan and Apollo.

FLANKING TABLE:

The candlestands were made in London in 1676, probably at the same time as the mirror above, which is not hallmarked.

ON TABLE IN FRONT OF BAY WINDOW:

The toilet set was made in London in 1673, and purchased by the 1st Duke at the sale following the death of his grandmother, the Countess of Northampton, 70 years later. It consists of a mirror, a pair of large circular bowls, scent jars and boxes of different sizes and shapes, hairbrushes, and a small silver eye-bath. The fashion for these costly toilet sets reached England during the Restoration, after 1660. This is the earliest silver toilet set of English make that is known to survive.

RIGHT OF BAY WINDOW:

The two series of small vases with concave sides, containing bunches of silver flowers, are believed to be early 17th-century Portuguese altar vases.

FLANKING BED:

The two small horizontal mirrors (sometimes known as sconces, since they were intended to reflect

candlelight) are French, *c.*1708, by the silversmith Pierre Dointrée of Paris.

LEFT OF CHIMNEYPIECE, ON EBONY CABINET:

The three large 'ginger jars', heavily embossed and fluted, are of the Charles II period. Their shape resembles that of a Chinese porcelain ginger jar – hence their rather misleading name. Like many of the contents of the King's Room, such extravagant objects were intended for display rather than use, emphasising the luxury of a state bedroom. The other two jars, *c.*1685–90, are engraved with birds and animals in a remarkably early chinoiserie style.

FLANKING CHIMNEYPIECE:

The silver sconces, or wall-lights, bear the arms of Sackville and Compton, and celebrate the marriage of the 6th Earl and his second wife, Mary Compton, daughter of the 3rd Earl of Northampton, in 1685.

OTHER FURNITURE

LEFT OF CHIMNEYPIECE:

The large ebony cabinet, with carved door-panels representing the story of Jonah and the Whale, was probably made in Paris about 1650 and was another of the 6th Earl's 'perquisites' from Whitehall.

PICTURE

ABOVE CHIMNEYPIECE:

287 *James I* (1566–1625)
After PAUL VAN SOMER (*c.*1576–1621)

THE LEAD STAIRCASE

The treads of the staircase that leads down from the far end of the Cartoon Gallery to the Stone Court are covered in lead.

FURNITURE

The oak longcase clock is English and was made in the first half of the 18th century.

The silver toilet set in the King's Room was made in 1673 and acquired by the 1st Duke for Knole 70 years later

CHAPTER TWO
THE PARK AND GARDEN

On display in the Great Hall is a facsimile of the bound manuscript of Virginia Woolf's novel *Orlando*. The novel is dedicated to Vita Sackville-West and, in the words of Vita's son Nigel Nicolson, who donated the manuscript to the National Trust, it is 'the longest and most charming love-letter in literature'. Vita is the eponymous hero/heroine (Orlando changes sex over the four centuries in which the novel is set), and Orlando's ancestral home is a house, like Knole, with a legendary 365 rooms:

There it lay in the early sunshine of spring [reads one passage which particularly moved Vita]. It looked a town rather than a house, but a town built, not hither and thither, as this man wished or that, but circumspectly, by a single architect with one idea in his head. Courts and buildings, grey, red, plum colour, lay orderly and symmetrical ... here was a chapel, there a belfry; spaces of the greenest grass lay in between and clumps of cedar trees and beds of bright flowers; all were clasped – yet so well set out was it that it seemed that every part had room to spread itself fittingly – by the roll of a massive wall; while smoke from innumerable chimneys curled perpetually into the air.

The pages are threaded through with similarly specific references to Knole and to its past and present incumbents: the head gardener Stubbs, Vita's father's elkhound Canute, and so on.

Orlando ends in the present day – indeed, on the novel's publication day, 11 October 1928, when Orlando returns to Knole to welcome a great Queen to the house. This was also the year of Vita's father's death; and the novel allows Vita, as Orlando, to take possession, in fantasy, of the house that she had been denied in fact. That, at least, was some compensation for Vita; for, as her husband, Harold Nicolson wrote to her, it was 'a book in which you and Knole are identified for ever'.

KNOLE PARK

On her return to Knole in 1928, Orlando drives in a motor-car:

up the curving drive between the elms and oaks through the falling turf of the park whose fall was so gentle that had it been water it would have spread the beach with a smooth green tide. Planted here and in solemn groups were beech trees and oak trees ... All this, the trees, deer and turf, she observed with the greatest satisfaction as if her mind had become fluid that flowed around things and enclosed them completely. Next time she drew up in the courtyard where, for so many hundred years, she had come, on horseback or in coach and six, with men riding before or coming after ...

In *Orlando*, time skips, then stands still, then starts again. The sense of timelessness evoked in the novel is nowhere more keenly felt than in the park, because here the fictional romance is matched by reality. Knole Park is one of very few deer-parks in England to have survived the past 500 years (there were some 700 in the 16th century) – and the only one in Kent.

The park was first enclosed by a fence in 1456 by Thomas Bourchier to indulge a passion, popular among the nobility, for hunting. Dry valleys that mark the course of a long-vanished river run for miles around the park; and it was along these – and across the plains above – that the deer, once dislodged from the woodlands, would be chased by greyhounds into paddocks or nets, where the kill would take place. Those who wanted a bird's-eye view of the brutality could stand on one of the two hills, one at the south-east of the park, known as the Mast Head, and the other at the west, called Echo Mount. Gervase Markham, the writer on countryside matters, could have been describing the topography of Knole when, in 1616, he wrote about Tudor deer-hunting:

(Right) The deer-park

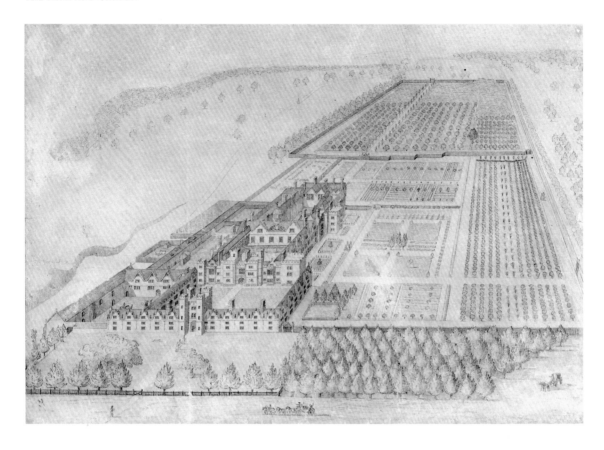

A bird's-eye view of Knole from the west in the early 18th century; drawing by Leonard Knyff

... the hills which are commonly called the viewes or discoveries of parkes, would bee all goodly high woods of tall timber, as well for the beauty and grace-fulnesse of the parke, as also for the echoe and sound which will rebound from the same, when in times of hunting, either the cries of the hounds, the winding of hornes, or the gibbetting of the huntsmen passeth through the same, doubling the musicke, and making it tenne times more delightfulle.

In some ways the Tudor deer-park marked a transition between the medieval game forest and the more ornamental parks of the 17th and 18th centuries. Elements of the medieval landscape survive in the hawthorn, oak, yew, hornbeam, silver birch, bird maple and ash trees that once dominated the woodlands of the Weald. And it is these that contribute to the timelessness of the park: to the fact

that it has changed little since Thomas Sackville's death in 1608.

During the 16th and 17th centuries, timber from the park was sold to the shipyards at Chatham; wood was coppiced for hop-poles and for fuel for the local glass industry; some of the land was given over for grazing; and some ploughed for growing crops. But the soils were thin, and the park remained substantially unchanged.

During the 18th century, many landowners decided to 'improve' their parks, employing designers such as 'Capability' Brown or Humphry Repton to create self-consciously picturesque land-scapes: 'We precisely mean by it,' wrote William Gilpin in 1798, 'that kind of beauty which would look well in a picture.' Knole, however, largely escaped this type of treatment – partly because the deer themselves already made the place look orna-mental enough, and partly because of the same innate conservatism of the Sackville family that has led to the house remaining relatively untouched, too, over the centuries.

The only concessions to 18th-century taste were the planting of stands of beech, and broad tree-lined avenues in place of the old coppiced woodlands. Two of these avenues, the Chestnut Walk and the Broad Walk (beech and oak), converge on the Mast Head in the south-east corner of the park, while the Duchess Walk (oak) leads northwards away from the house. Some of the buildings in the park reflect the 18th-century passion for the picturesque: the fake ruins, built in the 1760s a couple of hundred yards to the east of the main garden, for example, were designed presumably to indulge 'that pleasing melancholy musing which is always excited at the view of such venerable moments of departed grandeur'. The octagonal Gothic Revival Bird House was another folly, built nearby around 1761, perhaps incorporating genuinely medieval stone-work from Otford Palace. Less fanciful, however, were the walled kitchen garden, laid out in 1710–11, and an ice-house, which now forms a

mound towards the top of the knoll on which the house stands and from which it takes its name.

During both World Wars, areas of the park were used for military camps. But apart from the metalled roads built by the army and the bomb craters beside the golf course, which commemorate Knole's site astride 'Bomb Alley' between London and the Channel, there was little change. The 600-odd herd of deer continued to crop the turf between the hummocky ant-hills, the lighter-coloured fallow deer joined, since the 19th century, by the darker, shorter, stockier Japanese Sika deer.

The great storm of October 1987 wreaked real devastation. In the course of one night, nearby Sevenoaks lost all but one of its seven commemorative oaks; and 70 per cent of the trees in the park – exposed on a lofty sandstone ridge – were lost. The fact that many of these trees were some 200 years old had made them particularly vulnerable to the 100mph winds, but the storm also created an opportunity. Over the next five years, on the initiative of the 6th Lord Sackville, enthusiastic plantation-

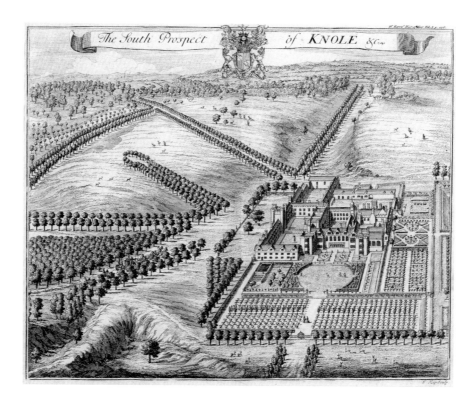

The park from the south in the early 18th century; engraving by Jan Kip

Knole from the north-west in the late 18th century; watercolour by Paul Sandby

clearer and passionate lover of the park, the 1,000 acres were replanted at the cost of £1 million, of which Sackville family trusts contributed one half and grants the other half.

There had never before been a formal design for Knole Park, and it was exactly this which had made it unique. The plan for replanting, therefore, had to be extremely unobtrusive, since its aim was to return the park delicately to its former condition: unplanned, except for a few strategic sight-lines.

THE GARDEN

There has been a garden at Knole for 500 years, ever since the days of Archbishop Bourchier, who created a small medieval lavender garden and an orchard near to the house. In the 16th century, under the ownership of Henry VIII and, later, during the tenancy of the Lennard family, this was extended, and the Kentish ragstone walls, which run for almost a mile around the 24-acre garden, were added. Punctuating the walls is a series of wrought-iron gates, mostly dating from the time of the 6th Earl at the end of the 17th century. Through these gates are views out of and into the garden.

Then as now, the garden was divided into a formal area, with lawns and borders, and an infor-

mal area known as the Wilderness (mentioned by Lady Anne Clifford in her diary in the early 17th century), where mossy paths wind their way under the beech trees. Like the park, the Wilderness was devastated by the storm of 1987. This area of the garden has been replanted, too – to a design which respected the spirit of the past. Several of the avenues, which had been created towards the end of the 17th century by the 5th Earl, were retained.

Leonard Knyff and Jan Kip's bird's-eye-view engraving, in *Britannia Illustrata* (1707), shows a formal walled garden, which was laid out in squares and rectangles, primarily as orchard. The royal gardener George London supplied fruit trees in 1698 and may have been responsible for the design. In 1709 the 1st Duke turned to a Westminster gardener, Thomas Ackers, who seems to have introduced the considerable changes visible in Thomas Badeslade's view of 1719. Badeslade records an oval bowling green with topiary arbours to the south of the house and a complex parterre to the east. In the early 18th century, a Dutch canal was built where the sunken pond (now swimming-pool) is; hot-houses for growing pineapples were built beside the chapel in the late 18th century, during the time of the 3rd Duke; seats and a small summer-house were added in the early 19th century (around the time that the Orangery was made); and the rhododendrons, the knot garden and some of the herbaceous borders date from Victorian times.

CHAPTER THREE
THE PALACE (1456–1566)

From the outside, Knole looks much the same today as it did in 1608, after a century and a half of intensive building had transformed a late medieval house into one of the largest country houses in Britain. Its grey ragstone bulk, sprawling over four acres, without any overall attempt at symmetry, had been created by a succession of different owners. These included Archbishops of Canterbury, Henry VIII and Thomas Sackville, the first of many generations of the Sackville family to live in the house.

ARCHBISHOP BOURCHIER'S BUILDINGS

To get a sense of Knole's early history – of what its first owners built and why – the best place to start is within the main entrance, in the Green Court. Straight ahead is Bourchier's Tower, one of the oldest parts of the house. This was the original gatehouse to an archbishop's palace. In 1456 Thomas Bourchier, Archbishop of Canterbury, had bought the manor of Knole from Sir William Fiennes, Lord Say and Sele, for £266 13s 4d. The manor consisted of several hundred acres that had been acquired from smallholders over the previous century and then let to tenants. But no one is sure what Knole itself looked like before Bourchier's purchase – or, indeed, in the absence of any firm evidence above ground, whether a building was already on the site.

Bourchier continued to cajole and coerce local farmers into selling up, creating an estate that, in an age of higher rents, could support the building and repair of a great house. By the second half of the 15th century, noblemen were building houses with domestic comfort rather than military defence in mind. Many of the architectural features of the medieval castle survived – in particular, the auster-

ity of the massive walls. But no boiling oil would ever have been poured from the turrets that decorated Bourchier's new gatehouse. And the large, carefully carved stone oriel window of his oratory, projecting above the entrance, was never designed to deter attackers.

Beyond the gatehouse, enclosing three sides of what is now the Stone Court, Bourchier built two-storeyed timber galleries, which acted as corridors connecting the gatehouse with the Great Hall.

(Right) Bourchier's Tower

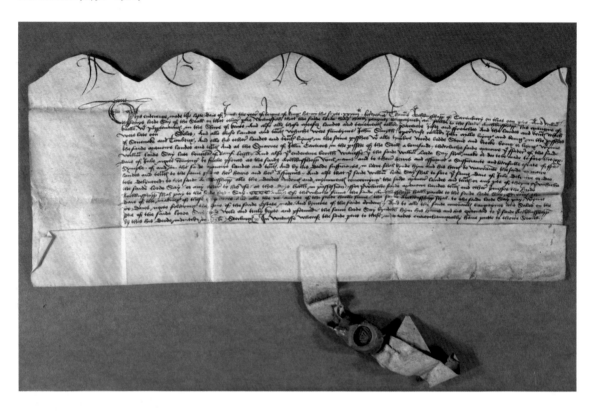

The deed of sale of Knole from Lord Say and Sele to Archbishop Bourchier, 30 June 1456

DINING IN STATE
(THE GREAT HALL AND GREAT CHAMBER)

Built around 1460, Bourchier's Great Hall proclaimed the grandeur of a senior officer of church and state, who crowned Edward IV in 1461, officiated at the coronation of Richard III in 1483, and married Henry VII to Elizabeth of York in 1486. The room was even taller then – before a ceiling was installed in the early 17th century beneath Bourchier's lofty timber roof. It was here that the Archbishop entertained on special occasions, such as weddings and funerals, and where his own household – the stewards and gentlemen servants, the bakers and brewers, the craftsmen and choirboys – took their meals every day.

At Christmas, for example, Bourchier would have made a show of 'good lordship' by entertaining his tenants in the Great Hall. No records of Bourchier's hospitality at Knole survive, but it is quite possible to recreate such occasions from the etiquette books and manuals of good housekeeping of the time. On a dais facing the room, the lord and his closest associates would have dined at a table covered with a linen damask table-cloth and strewn with fragrant herbs and flowers. In the middle of the top table stood an ornate salt cellar that separated the favoured few from the other guests, who perched on stools – in strict order of status – at trestle-tables up and down the length of the hall; hence, the expressions 'above' and 'below the salt'. Beside the top table were 'cupboards', or tables, piled with valuable silver.

When everything was ready, the lord and his guests took their seats at the top table. With much ceremony, the top of the salt cellar was removed by an attendant, the other guests took their places, and a Latin grace was said. The lord's steward then led a procession of dishes to the table. Each of the three courses would have consisted of up to 20 dishes. Roast lamb and fowl, carved in front of the lord and served with a peppery vinegar-based sauce, might have been followed by a variety of pies and by venison, served with 'frumenty' made from wheat boiled in spiced milk; the dessert course, served on special occasions, might have included fruit and wafers accompanied by sweet wine. Elaborately sculptured confections of sugar and almond paste, known as 'subtilties', were served between each course. Archbishop Warham's enthronement ceremony in Canterbury in 1504 featured 'Saint Eustace kneeling in a Park under a great tree full of roses'.

Catering for several hundred diners required a large kitchen. On one side of the passage leading to the Great Hall at Knole, doors open on to a pantry (from the French *paneterie*, or bread store), where bread was kept, and on to a buttery (from the French *bouteillerie*, or bottle store), where the butler dispensed wine, ale and cider. The passage continues to a servery and to an old kitchen almost as large as the hall itself (which might have been the hall of an earlier manor house). Here the clerk of the kitchen commanded a large army of cooks and other servants, who slept at night on straw pallets on the stone-flagged floor.

A century before, a great magnate such as Bourchier might have presided daily over his retainers in the Great Hall, but by the late 15th century there was a gradual withdrawal by the grandees into more private areas. This social trend was reflected in the architecture of the day. Bourchier's main reception room, or Great Chamber, was on the first floor (where the Ballroom now is), with a parlour below, and was reached by a stairway from the Great Hall. Here the Archbishop would have entertained visiting dignitaries. Despite the greater comfort and privacy of the surroundings, there would have been no less ceremony. The dinner would still have been brought by a procession of servants through the hall and up the staircase. As the marshal of the hall shouted 'By your leave, masters', all the retainers who were waiting for their own meal in the Great Hall stood up and watched in silence as the dishes for the lord's table were paraded past.

From the Great Chamber, a door led to the Archbishop's private apartments in a new tower (now known as the Duke's Tower) that Bourchier

built around 1467. There was easy access from here to a private pew overlooking the chapel, Bourchier's other major contribution to the building of Knole. The chapel lay in the south-eastern corner of Bourchier's palace, and was reached at ground-floor level by a covered walk from the Great Hall.

FROM ARCHBISHOP'S PALACE TO ROYAL RESIDENCE

Bourchier died at Knole in 1486, bequeathing the house to the See of Canterbury. Knole then passed to John Morton, Bourchier's successor as Archbishop of Canterbury and, as a result, stayed close to the heart of Tudor politics. It was in 1487, during

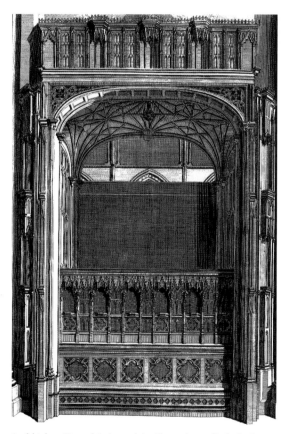

Archbishop Bourchier's tomb in Canterbury Cathedral; engraving from John Dart's History and Antiquities of the Cathedral Church of Canterbury *(1726). This was to be the inspiration for Horace Walpole's Gallery at Strawberry Hill*

his ownership of Knole, that Morton devised the great 'Catch 22' of Tudor times – 'Morton's Fork'. In an attempt to raise loans to pay for Henry VII's war in France, Morton presented reluctant lenders with the following dilemma:

If the persons applied to for benevolence [forced loan] live frugally, tell them that their parsimony must have enriched them, and the king will therefore expect from them a liberal donation. If their method of living on the contrary be extravagant, tell them that they can afford to give largely, since the proof of their opulence is evident by their expenditure.

Morton's own wealth, however, was undiminished by such demands. He could afford to enlarge Bourchier's building, and so – after his death at Knole in 1500 – could his successor but one, William Warham, Archbishop of Canterbury from 1504 to 1532. It was probably between 1486 and 1532 that buildings, later destroyed by a fire in 1623, were added to the east of the house, beside the chapel. These private apartments were connected to the Great Hall by means of what is now the Brown Gallery and part of what is now the Leicester Gallery. The galleries were more than mere corridors linking the scattered buildings and gradually causing the sprawling house to coalesce; they also provided a brief pause – a form of reception area – half-way between the public and the private rooms.

In 1538 Thomas Cranmer, the author of the Book of Common Prayer who had succeeded Warham as Archbishop in 1532, was forced 'voluntarily' to give Knole to Henry VIII. Cranmer's secretary Ralph Morice recalled the interview between the reluctant archbishop and the acquisitive King:

I was by when Otford [another of the Archbishop's palaces, three miles away] and Knole was given him. My lord [Cranmer], minding to have retained Knole unto himself, said that it was too small a house for his majesty. 'Marry', (said the king), 'I had rather have it than this house (meaning Otford), for it standeth on a better soil. This house standeth low, and is rheumatick, like unto Croydon, where I could never be without sickness. And as for Knole [it] standeth on a sound, perfect, wholesome ground. And if I should make mine abode here, as I do surely mind to do now and then, I myself will lie at Knole, and most of my house[hold] shall lie at Otford.' And so by this means

both those houses were delivered up into the king's hands.....

Henry VIII probably did not spend much time at Knole – after all, he had acquired a total of 60 royal residences by the time of his death. But there is evidence that he spent a certain amount of money on the house: £872 in 1543 and £80 in 1546. Some of this was given to the steward of the manor, Sir Richard Long, 'for making the King's garden at Knole'. But most of it seems to have gone on building the new gatehouse, which is now the main entrance to Knole, and on erecting the buildings around the Green Court. Henry may have built on to Bourchier's gatehouse, extending the façade to include the new King's Tower at the southern corner and a small, entirely ornamental turret at the northern. Ranged around the Green Court, rather like a courtyard at Hampton Court or the quadrangle of an Oxbridge college of a similar date, were sets of rooms, each reached by individual stairways, to house the King's retinue whenever he came to visit. On the north side of the Green Court were the King's Stables, where the master of horse and the equerries were accommodated. This range overlooked the stables themselves on the other side.

After the death of Henry VIII in 1547, Knole passed to his ten-year-old son Edward VI, who in 1550 granted it to his guardian or Protector, John Dudley, Duke of Northumberland. When Northumberland was executed on the accession of Queen Mary in 1553, the new queen assigned the house (where, as a princess, she had spent six months as Cranmer's guest in 1533) to Cardinal Pole, Cranmer's successor as Archbishop of Canterbury. After Mary's death, Queen Elizabeth granted Knole in 1561 to Northumberland's son and her favourite, Robert Dudley, later Earl of Leicester. Leicester may have made alterations to parts of the house and, in particular, the eastern side where a gallery is named after him. But after five years in his possession, he handed Knole back to the Queen in exchange for a large grant of land elsewhere. In the meantime, however, Leicester had assigned a 99-year lease on Knole to one Thomas Rolf, who left his estate to John Dudley and William Lovelace, and then promptly died.

The west front was probably built for Henry VIII between 1543 and 1547

CHAPTER FOUR
KNOLE AND THOMAS SACKVILLE
(1566–1608)

The ownership of Knole in the years following Leicester's occupation is rather shadowy. Tradition has it that Elizabeth I gave Knole to her cousin and councillor, Thomas Sackville, 'to keep him near her court and councils that he might repair thither, in any emergency'. But there is no documentary evidence for such a gift; and, in any case, the Queen was notorious for her parsimony. The maze of property negotiations leading to Thomas Sackville's ownership of Knole conceals a less romantic story, but one that is perhaps a truer reflection of Sackville's character and the politics of the age.

THE SACKVILLE FAMILY

Thomas Sackville was 30 years old when Leicester returned Knole to the Queen in 1566. Like most ambitious families of the time, the Sackvilles claimed that they had come to England with William the Conqueror, before settling first in Buckinghamshire and then at Buckhurst in Sussex. Thomas's grandfather John Sackville had married Anne Boleyn's aunt Margaret, which made Thomas a second cousin – and therefore one of the closest relatives – of Queen Elizabeth on her accession to the throne in 1558. His father Richard had been an extremely successful lawyer, businessman and courtier. As Chancellor of the Court of Augmentations, which administered the estates of the dissolved monasteries, Richard exploited the lucrative opportunities afforded by public office (as future generations of the family were to do). This earned him a fortune – and the nickname 'Fillsack'.

Gradually the Sackvilles acquired greater estates in Sussex and Kent. Many of these derived their income from the sale of timber to the Wealden iron industry, which used charcoal to fuel its blast furnaces. Richard Sackville also invested directly in ironworks, profited from the production of cast-iron guns, and even dabbled in arms dealing.

Like his father, Thomas trained as a lawyer, but he was also a distinguished poet. In 1561, when he was 25, his first play, *Gorboduc* – one of the earliest English blank-verse tragedies – was performed in front of the Queen herself. 'Full of stately speeches and well-sounding phrases,' according to Sir Philip Sidney, it is little read today, although scholars view it as a minor landmark in English literature and an influence on Spenser and Shakespeare. On his father's death in 1566, Thomas Sackville inherited a large fortune and a country house at Buckhurst, and in 1567 he was made Baron Buckhurst – one of only two completely new peerages created by Elizabeth. His career as a courtier was taking off, and in 1570 – at the age of 34 – he acquired a lease on Knole from John Dudley and William Lovelace for £1,000 each.

THE BUYING AND SELLING OF KNOLE

Two years earlier, Sackville had entertained a party of French Huguenots, who had fled religious persecution, including Odet de Coligny, whose portrait (no. 4) hangs in the Great Hall. In a letter to the Privy Council, he attempted to excuse himself from accusations of less than splendid hospitality:

I brought them [the Huguenots] in to every part of the house [the royal mansion at Shene] that I possessed, and showed them all such stuff and furniture as I had. And where they required plate of me, I told them as troth is, that I had no plate at all. Such glass vessels as I had I offered them, which they thought too base; for napery I could not satisfy their turn, for they desired damask work for a long table, and I had none other but plain linen for a square table. The table whereon I dine myself I offered them, and for that it was a square table

Thomas Sackville, 1st Earl of Dorset (1536–1608), Lord Treasurer to Queen Elizabeth. He took possession of Knole in 1603, and during the last years of his life magnificently extended and embellished the house. Painting attributed to John de Critz (no. 1; Great Hall)

they refused it. One only tester and bedstead not occupied I had, and those I delivered for the Cardinal himself, and when we could not by any means in so short a time procure another bedstead for the bishop, I assigned them the bedstead on which my wife's waiting women did lie, and laid them on the ground. Mine own basin and ewer I lent to the Cardinal and wanted myself.

His finances were further drained by serving as ambassador to France in 1571–2. He economised by assigning the lease of Knole in 1574 to John Lennard, a local landowner, whose family occupied the house for the next 30 years and were probably responsible for creating the large walled garden. In 1604, however, Thomas Sackville bought back the lease on Knole (which still had another 61 years to run) from Lennard's son, Sampson, for £4,000. On 5 April 1605 the Crown, which still owned the freehold on the property, sold this to Rowland White and others for £220 6s 8d; and two days later, Sackville bought it off them for £2,500. Thomas Sackville had become the freehold owner of Knole – without the encumbrance of any sitting tenants. What lay behind this labyrinth of property deals?

By 1605 Thomas Sackville had rebuilt his family fortunes, partly through income from the sale of timber to ironworks and to the builders of houses and ships. He had consolidated his position by years of loyal service to the Crown in national and local government, for which he was rewarded by a string of appointments and titles – as a Privy Counsellor (1586), a Knight of the Garter (1589), Chancellor of the Univeristy of Oxford (1591) and Earl of Dorset (1604). But, most significantly of all, he had in 1599 been made Lord Treasurer (the equivalent of Chancellor of the Exchequer today) by Queen Elizabeth, and been reappointed by James I soon after his succession in 1603, which Sackville himself had helped to ensure.

One of Sackville's responsibilities as Lord Treasurer was the sale of Crown lands. Had he negotiated the sale of the freehold of Knole directly to himself, he might have aroused the suspicions of the King and the envy of his colleagues. But by authorising the sale to Rowland White and others, and then buying it back off them, he covered the paper trail with a thin veil of propriety.

Such transactions – the 'gleanings and purloinings of the Old Treasurer', according to one contemporary – were commonplace and accepted in Tudor and Stuart politics. Before the 19th century, when a sense of the duty and responsibility of public office became the norm, it was more usual to think not of what you could do for your country, but what it could do for you. In the words of Edmund Spenser, writing about a courtier in 1590:

For to increase the common treasure's store;
But his own treasure he increased more . . .

As well as the sale of Crown lands, senior courtiers could hope to benefit from the administration of monopolies for goods such as soap or starch or, as Thomas Sackville did from 1604, from the administration of the Great Customs Farm, which collected almost all the customs duty for the country in exchange for guaranteeing the Crown an annual rent.

The lead rainwater pipes in the Stone Court are decorated with the 1st Earl's initials, coronet and Garter

By 1605, Thomas Sackville, 1st Earl of Dorset was 69 years old. According to his son, he had needed a 'place near London to retire into', particularly since the Court now spent more and more time in and around the capital. He suffered from rheumatism, and the roads that led through the 'miry vale' of the Weald to his house at Buckhurst in Sussex were rutted by carts carrying iron and timber. Coaches regularly got bogged down in mud, produced by the rain that flowed from the Downs on either side. In 1601 Sackville had also taken a lease on West Horsley Place in Surrey and made this his main country abode. But his plans for Knole were more ambitious. They were designed to announce the final arrival of a family whose spectacular successes over the past century had made it one of the wealthiest in England. In the words of the 17th-century statesman and philosopher Francis Bacon, 'when men sought to cure mortality by fame . . . buildings were the only way'.

THE REMAKING OF KNOLE

With the exception of some glazing work carried out during the Lennards' tenancy, Knole was probably quite dilapidated by the time Thomas Sackville acquired the property for good. In the tradition of other Tudor and Stuart Lord Treasurers, he set about creating a great showhouse – financed by the fruits of his high office. William Cecil, Queen Elizabeth's Treasurer, had built Theobalds in Hertfordshire and Burghley House in Lincolnshire, and his son Robert, who succeeded Sackville as Lord Treasurer, rebuilt Hatfield House in Hertfordshire. Indeed, the magnificence of Audley End in Essex, a palace built by a later Lord Treasurer, the Earl of Suffolk, prompted King James I to observe wryly that 'it was too big for a king but fitting for a Lord Treasurer'.

From 1604 painters and plasterers, woodcarvers and stonemasons were brought by Thomas Sackville to Knole. Many of these master craftsmen were employed by the King's Works department, which was under the control of the Lord Treasurer (although paid for on private business by Sackville himself). He wanted to soften the massive severity of the house, to bring touches of the modern age to

his medieval home – but most of all, he wanted to proclaim to the world his personal wealth and status as a senior statesman. Stone leopards carrying the family coat of arms sprang from gables all over the house; and the Sackville arms surmounted by an earl's coronet, with the initials TD (Thomas Dorset) and the date 1605, adorned the lead downpipes that directed rain-water into cisterns in the courtyards.

Sixteenth-century ideas about the structure of the universe and the natural order of things were reflected in architecture in a respect for symmetry and proportion. To add an impression of symmetry and order to the west façade, which incorporated in rather ramshackle fashion Bourchier's original gatehouse and Henry VIII's towers, Thomas Sackville added a two-storeyed bay, topped with a gable, on either side of Bourchier's Tower. He enclosed the timber galleries around three sides of the Stone Court and faced them with stone, and at the far end of the courtyard he added a Doric colonnade to disguise the fact that the passage leading to the Great Hall was – as with most medieval halls – off-centre. On the south front (beneath the Cartoon Gallery and visible from the garden), he built a colonnade with seven marble arches – to create an elegant, ordered façade. This Renaissance aspect to the house contrasts strikingly with the simple severity of Henry VIII's west front and with the looming bulk of the north front, where the outbuildings – a barn, an old brew-house, a granary, and workshops for carpenters, bricklayers and painters – cluster higgledy-piggledy beneath the Clock Tower, like the yards and farm buildings of a medieval village.

Whatever his taste for Renaissance ornamentation and decoration, Thomas Sackville maintained many aspects of the late medieval way of life. Behind the newly symmetrical façades, the ways in which the rooms were arranged differed little from Bourchier's day.

One obituarist claimed that 'for more than twenty years, beside workmen and other hired,' the number of Thomas Sackville's household 'at the least hath been two hundred and twenty daily, as appeared upon check-role. A very rare example in this present age of ours, when housekeeping is so decayed.' Nowhere was the scale of the household more apparent than in the Great Hall, where the

retainers would have continued to eat on most days, with the family seated on the dais on high days and holidays. To accommodate his servants, Sackville had a decorated plasterwork ceiling erected beneath the beams of Bourchier's tall timber roof, thereby creating a new attic space – the Retainers' Gallery – above the Great Hall. He also had an oak screen at one end carved with caryatids and heraldic devices by William Portington, which may originally have been brightly painted and gilded. The lattice windows at the top of this concealed a musicians' gallery, where a small orchestra would have performed to the guests below.

Thomas Sackville intended to 'keep his state' and do most of his entertaining, like Bourchier, in the Great Chamber (now the Ballroom). However, something more impressive than Bourchier's small – probably spiral – staircase at the far end of the Great Hall was needed to convey the visitor there. So Thomas Sackville commissioned a new and much grander wooden staircase, built around an open stairwell, leading off the Great Hall. In true classical style, the three flights of steps are supported by Doric columns at the bottom, Ionic in the middle, and Corinthian at the top. Every surface of the Great Staircase is covered with paintings of *The Four Ages of Man*, *The Five Senses* and Virtues and Vices, which described a spiritual progress through life (see p. 14).

The Great Chamber was the *pièce de résistance*. Here, the craftsmen of the King's Works installed a plasterwork ceiling (by Richard Dungan), carved panelling and a frieze around the walls (by Portington), and a magnificent marble and alabaster chimneypiece (by Cornelius Cure). The carved musical instruments above the fireplace suggest that this was a room for music, dancing and masques as well as for eating.

Like Bourchier, the lord and his family would usually have retired to the Withdrawing Room next door (now the Reynolds Room) for meals and privacy. But on grander occasions, they would have escorted a particularly distinguished guest in a ceremonial procession along the Cartoon Gallery

(Left) The chimneypiece in the Great Chamber (now Ballroom)

Richard Dungan's plasterwork ceiling in the Cartoon Gallery features plants probably taken from a herbal

(with its floorboards then covered in rush matting) to the principal bedchamber, the King's Room. As the name suggests, this was designed to accommodate James I should he visit Knole.

A STATELY ASCENT

In many ways, a visitor to Knole today follows the same route as a grandee of the early 17th century: sweeping along the main axis of the house through two apparently symmetrical courtyards, the Green Court and the Stone Court, into the Great Hall, before processing up the Great Staircase to the door of the Great Chamber and along a parade of galleries and withdrawing rooms to the principal bedroom suites. Two other galleries apart from the Cartoon Gallery led from the Great Chamber to suites of rooms, comprising a bedchamber and a closet, for visiting dignitaries: the Brown Gallery to the Spangle Bedroom and Dressing Room, and the Leicester Gallery to the Venetian Ambassador's Room and Dressing Room (now Museum Room).

Thomas Sackville died in 1608 at the Privy Council table in Whitehall. He had had very little time to enjoy for himself the transformation that he had initiated at Knole.

CHAPTER FIVE
THE 17TH CENTURY

On his death in 1608, Thomas Sackville was succeeded as Earl of Dorset by his son Robert, who died in 1609, and then by his grandson, Richard. Thanks to a diary written by Richard's wife, Anne Clifford, we have an intimate account of everyday life at Knole in the early 17th century.

THE KNOLE DIARY

One of the reasons why Anne wrote this diary was to record her attempts to protect what she regarded as her inheritance both from her Clifford relations and from the predatory attentions of her husband. When Anne's father, George Clifford, 3rd Earl of Cumberland, had died in 1605, he left his extensive estates in Yorkshire to his younger brother Francis. This was in direct contravention of a deed drawn up almost 300 years before, which provided that these estates should pass from parent to child, regardless of sex. Anne and her widowed mother, Margaret, therefore believed that this land was Anne's. Furthermore, the Clifford estates in Westmorland – and, in particular, the four castles at Appleby, Brougham, Brough and Pendragon – had in 1593 been granted, as part of her marriage settlement, to Margaret for her lifetime.

Richard and Anne were both nineteen years old when they married in 1609. It was a perfect match between two great dynasties, one from the south, the other from the north of England – and it had partly been arranged by Richard's grandfather, Thomas, before his death. Anne was happy at first. Her husband was a close friend of Henry, Prince of Wales and, according to her account, 'in his owne Nature of a just mynde, of a sweet Disposition, and verie valiant in his owne person'. But he was also very extravagant, exhibiting great 'prodigality in housekeeping, and other noble ways at court, as tilting, masqueing, and the like'. She constantly refers in the diaries to his gadding-about – to hunting, greyhound racing, gambling ('losing 400 pieces playing with the King') and cockfighting. Later on in their marriage, there are some rather sad, understated references to his mistresses.

In the Ballroom there is a full-length painting of Richard Sackville, 3rd Earl of Dorset attributed to William Larkin. With his jutting elbow and his hand resting nonchalantly on his hip, in a manner so typical of 16th- and 17th-century portraiture, he projects a certain swagger. The clothes of this popinjay are magnificent, too. An inventory of his wardrobe, made in 1617, records over a hundred items, ranging from velvet cloaks and doublets made of cloth of gold to green silk stockings and gloves 'embroidered with suns, moons & stars and edged with gold & silver lace'. These are the clothes which Lady Anne records in her diary as being cut up to provide fabric for chairs and stools at Knole.

Unlike his wife, Richard had no emotional attachment to the Clifford estates in the north, and was interested in his wife's claims to them only to the extent that they could generate enough cash to fund his way of life or ward off his creditors. As Anne's lawsuit with her Clifford relations ground through the courts, she came under increasing pressure from her husband to agree to a cash settlement, in return for forsaking all claim to the northern estates. At various times, Richard threatened her with separation, sent messages stating that she was no longer to live at Knole, and even used her daughter Margaret as a pawn, having her taken away from Anne. 'At first,' she wrote, '[this] was somewhat grievous to me, but when I considered that it would both make my Lord more angry with me & be worse for the Child, I resolved to let her go.'

Not surprisingly, all this put a great strain on their marriage, and her life at Knole is a litany of emotional ups and downs:

Lady Anne Clifford (1590–1676), who married Richard, 3rd Earl of Dorset in 1609; attributed to William Larkin

All the time I stayed in the country I was sometimes merry and sometimes sad ... sometimes I had fair words from him and sometimes foul ... All this time my Lord was in London where he had all and infinite great resort coming to him. He went much abroad to Cocking, to Bowling Alleys, to Plays and Horse Races & [was] commended by all the World. I stayed in the Countrey having many times a sorrowful & heavy Heart & being condemned by most folks because I would not consent to the Agreement, so as I may truly say, I am like an Owl in the Desert.

She was particularly bitter about Richard's favourite, Matthew Caldicott, whom she suspected of constant stirring: 'my Lord and I had a great falling out, Matthew continuing still to do me all the ill offices he could with my Lord.' She even recorded the nights that she and her husband slept together: 'This night my Lord should have lain with me but he and I fell out about matters.' Those matters – presumably concerning her inheritance – had become less acrimonious by the following day, because the next night they did sleep together.

INTERESTED PARTIES

Pressure to agree to a compromise over her inheritance came from other parties, besides her husband. In 1616 the Archbishop of Canterbury got involved: 'Much persuasion was used by him & all the Company, sometimes terrifying me and sometimes flattering me.' A month later, she still refused to compromise.

The situation changed somewhat on the death of Anne's mother, Margaret, later that year. The Westmorland estates had been settled on Margaret only for her lifetime, and on her death were due to pass to Francis Clifford. Faced with the prospect of a *fait accompli*, Richard supported his wife's claim to these estates. As the redoubtable Anne went north to stake her claim to her mother's property, the couple were temporarily reconciled. 'My Lord & I were never greater friends than at this time,' she recorded in her diary.

But the case of the Clifford inheritance had begun to catch the attention of even grander figures. In November 1616 Richard challenged Lord Clifford to a duel, and King James I himself intervened to

mediate. On 18 January 1617 the pair was summoned to a private audience with the King:

He persuaded us both to Peace, & to put the whole Matter wholly into his hands. Which my Lord consented to, but I beseech'd His Majesty to pardon me for that I would never part with Westmoreland while I lived upon any Condition whatsoever. ... Sometimes he used fair means & persuasions, & sometimes foul means, but I was resolved before so as nothing would move me.

Despite her protestations, the King made his judgement in March 1617. All the Clifford estates, including the Westmorland lands enjoyed by Anne's mother during her lifetime, were to pass to the Cliffords, and Richard was to receive a cash settlement of £20,000 in compensation from the Cliffords, payable in instalments.

DAILY LIFE AT KNOLE

By now, the 28-year-old Lady Anne was tired out and disappointed, yet determined to 'set as merry a face as I could upon a discontented Heart'. In July 1618 she lost a five-month-old son Thomas. She was ill and prone, as she did on Good Friday 1619, to fall into 'a great passion of weeping'. Knole remains the backdrop to her brooding melancholy and her 'many wearisome days'.

Her diary records how she passed the time among 'the marble pillars' that had become her prison: stitching cushions or playing cards (on one occasion, 'I had such ill luck that I resolved not to play in 3 months'), walking 'abroad' or saying her prayers in the garden. She read or was read to from books as diverse as Ovid's *Metamorphoses*, the Bible, Montaigne's *Plays*, and Mr Sandy's *Book about the government of the Turks*. And, from time to time, she took a bath, talked about religion or made a resolution to eat only fish on Fridays for the rest of the year. She recorded when 'Couch puppied in the morning', the teething troubles of her daughter Margaret – always referred to as 'the Child' (whose portrait by Paul Van Somer hangs in Lady Betty Germain's Dressing Room), and every little illness, including when she ate so much cheese that it made her sick. It was a range of interests and activities worthy of a woman whom the poet and Sevenoaks

RICHARD SACKVILL EARL OF DORSET

Richard, 3rd Earl of Dorset (1589–1624). As this portrait attributed to William Larkin (no. 233; Ballroom) makes clear, he had a passion for fine clothes

rector, John Donne, had described as being able to 'discourse of all things from Predestination to Slea Silk'.

But the wonder of the diary is that the rooms and places to which she refers are recognisable today. As a result, the diary brings vividly to life the workings of an early 17th-century household. For example, Lady Anne refers to dining in the warmth of the withdrawing room (now the Reynolds Room), particularly in winter. On 4 April 1617, however, she records: 'This day we began to leave the Little Room and dine and sup in the Great Chamber [now the Ballroom].' At a later date, her husband 'dined abroad in the Great Chamber and supped privately with me in the Drawing Chamber'. On another occasion, her husband was 'troubled with a Cough & was fain to lie in the Leicester Chamber [now the Venetian Ambassador's Room].' She also spent hours in the garden, sometimes playing a form of 'tag' called Burley-break 'upon the Green [the

Anne Clifford's daughter, Margaret, whom she referred to simply as 'the Child'; by Paul van Somer (Lady Betty Germain's Dressing Room)

raised lawn that is visible from the Second Painted Staircase]'.

Like the archbishops, Richard and his wife did most of their entertaining in the Great Chamber, except on feast days when they joined the rest of their household of over 100 dependants in the Great Hall. As the daily seating plan between 1613 and 1624 shows, middle-ranking servants, including the clerks of the kitchen, the slaughterman, the baker and brewer, the head gardener and groom, and the yeoman of the buttery and pantry sat at the Clerks' Table at the raised end of the hall. Ranged at right-angles to the Clerks' Table along the hall were three tables: the 'Long Table' (which still survives) for lower servants, such as footmen, a farrier and a falconer, a bird-catcher and a barber; a nursery table, and a laundrymaid's table. Finally, at the bottom of the hall, there was a table reserved for kitchen and scullery staff, for characters with names such as Diggory Dyer, Marfidy Snipt and John Morockoe, 'a Blackamoor'. The 21 most senior servants dined in a separate parlour below the Great Chamber; these included the chaplain, the steward, the Gentleman of the Horse and 'Mr Matthew Caldicott, my Lord's favourite'.

In 1624, at the age of 34, Richard, who had been ill for several years, died, according to the gossip John Chamberlain, of a 'surfeit of potatoes'. In just sixteen years, he had spent what his forefathers had taken a century to acquire. He had sold most of his estates, including much of Fleet Street and Holborn in London – and even Knole itself, which he rented back from a London businessman called Henry Smith for £100 a year. His debts stood at around £60,000.

Lady Anne had had another daughter, Isabella, in 1622, but, according to her diary, all three of her sons had 'died young at Knole when they were born'. In 1624 she left Knole, which had passed on her husband's death to Richard's younger brother, Edward – another man whom she distrusted intensely. Her patience and longevity paid off, when, in 1643, she inherited the Clifford estates on the death of Francis Clifford's son, Henry, without male heirs.

The Great Hall in the early 18th century, when the tables were still arranged much as they had been in Lady Anne Clifford's day

EDWARD SACKVILLE, 4TH EARL OF DORSET

In the Great Hall there is a portrait of Edward Sackville, 4th Earl of Dorset. The gleaming breastplate and helmet suggest a soldier, the scarlet doublet and embroidered ruffs a courtier, and the blue sash of the Order of the Garter with the Lord Chamberlain's key of office dangling from his waist signify a statesman. Here is a portrait of a Royalist at the time of the Civil War, of a man who had once claimed, with a fatal lack of understanding, that 'there was no fear of insurrection in this kingdom'.

To complete the swashbuckling image, there is Edward's heroic account of a duel – probably over a woman – that he had fought in the Netherlands in 1613 with Lord Bruce:

Then passion, having so weak an enemy to assail as my discretion, easily became victor ... and then in a meadow ankle deep in water, bidding farewell to our doublets, in our shirts we began to charge each other ... I easily became master of him laying on his back ... Bruce died on the spot.

On succeeding his brother as 4th Earl of Dorset in 1624, a more sober picture emerges. Edward set about buying back Knole and restoring the estate that Richard had all but ruined. His major sources of income were typical of a courtier of the day: a judicious marriage; speculation in the City, particularly in companies that exploited the opportunities offered by the New World; the profits of public office; and, finally, the assiduous management of his own lands. In 1612 he had married an heiress, Mary Curzon (whose portrait attributed to William Larkin hangs in the Ballroom). In 1623–4 he was Governor of the Somers Island Company; between 1629 and 1634 a Commissioner for settling Virginia; and in 1637 the author of a petition to King Charles I for 'certain islands on the south of New England,

Edward, 4th Earl of Dorset (?1589–1652); studio of Van Dyck (no. 3; Great Hall)

the exploitation of the New World, but also at home – for example, in collecting the extremely lucrative tax on coal. And it placed a lot of patronage at his disposal, which could then be converted into cash in the form of bribes and back-handers.

As a result, Edward could begin to pay off his brother's debts and even to add to the estate at Knole. Entertainment at Knole recovered some of its former grandeur. A bill of fare for a banquet at Knole on 3 July 1636 begins with the instructions: 'To perfume the room often in the meal with orange flower water upon a hot pan. To have fresh bowls in every corner and flowers tied upon them, and sweet briar, stock, gilly-flowers, pinks, wall-flowers and any other sweet flowers in glasses and

Mary Curzon (d.1645), who married the 4th Earl in 1612; attributed to William Larkin (no. 234; Ballroom)

viz. Long Island, Cole Island, Sandy Point, Hell Gates', which 'were lately delivered by some of your Majesty's subjects, and are not yet inhabited by any Christians. Prays a grant thereof, with like powers of government as have been granted for other plantations in America.'

Just as his grandfather, Thomas Sackville, had benefited from his office as Lord Treasurer, Edward Sackville profited by proximity to the King (indeed, his wife was governess to Charles I's sons). In 1628 he was made Lord Chamberlain to the Queen, Henrietta Maria; and in 1645–6 Lord Chamberlain to the King himself. This closeness secured Edward opportunities not just in

Lady Frances Cranfield (d.1687), painted by Van Dyck, probably shortly before her marriage to the 5th Earl in 1637 (no. 236; Ballroom)

pots in every window and chimney.' The menu that follows includes two courses of 33 dishes each.

Perhaps the house, which sometimes appears so sad and subdued in Lady Anne's diaries, had recaptured some of its former gaiety. The galleries at Knole, which had played such a ceremonial role in the house that Thomas Sackville remodelled, were now used for exercise and entertainment as well. For example, the billiard-table in a bay at the east end of the Leicester Gallery dates from the early 17th century. Hanging from a hole in the ceiling nearby was a rope attached to a dumb-bell in the attic above.

KNOLE DURING THE CIVIL WAR

The Civil War disrupted the gradual restoration of Knole's fortunes. By September 1642, the 4th Earl had joined the King, and the following month he fought at the Battle of Edgehill. Charles I's younger son, the future King James II, later recalled how Dorset had been ordered to remove him and his elder brother, the future King Charles II, to safety up the hill and out of the battle, but that Dorset had refused, saying that he would 'not be thought a coward for ever a king's son in Christendom'.

Edward was punished for his support of the Royalist cause by a pre-emptive raid on Knole by Parliamentary soldiers in 1642. A letter written by the steward at Knole to the Earl of Dorset itemises 'the hurte done at Knoll house the 14th daie of August 1642 by the companie of Horsemen brought by Coronell [Colonel] Sandys'. The Parliamentary soldiers took away five wagon-loads of arms, broke 40 locks, and did a certain amount of general damage, such as taking the plumes from the bed-tester and the cushion cases embroidered with satin and gold from 'my Lord's chamber'.

In 1643, according to a Parliamentary order that the estates of those who had helped the Royalist cause should be sequestrated, Knole and its lands around Sevenoaks were seized; the Committee of Sequestration for Kent even used Knole as its local headquarters. This, however, was only a temporary measure. In 1644 the Committee for the Advance of Money assessed the 4th Earl's contribution to

Parliament at £5,000 and, when he failed to pay this, they kept possession of his house (although they allowed his wife to remain at Knole), seized his goods, inventoried them, and then sold them in 1645. Most of the furniture and paintings collected at Knole in the first half of the 17th century, apart from the family portraits, were dispersed in this way. Worse was to follow. In 1645 the 4th Earl's younger son, also called Edward, was taken prisoner in a battle near Oxford, and murdered the following year by a Parliamentary soldier. Such was the personal and financial cost of the Civil War to many people that by the mid-1640s, there were many — including the 4th Earl — who were arguing for moderation and reconciliation. By 1650 Dorset had paid his fine, and was in full possession of his estates once more. He died two years later.

RICHARD SACKVILLE, 5TH EARL OF DORSET

Edward was succeeded by his son, Richard (whose portrait hangs in the Ballroom), in 1652. Like his father, the 5th Earl had married an heiress. Frances Cranfield (whose portrait by Van Dyck in the Ballroom was probably painted shortly before their wedding in 1637) was the daughter of Lionel, 1st Earl of Middlesex, who had been Lord Treasurer to James I and, like Thomas Sackville before him, had amassed a considerable estate in the process. His mansion, Copt Hall in Essex, housed fine collections of furniture and family portraits, much of which eventually came to Knole. These included portraits by Daniel Mytens of him and of his former master, James I, in the Leicester Gallery.

The 5th Earl began repairing the depredations of the Civil War and kept his servants in order: fines were imposed for various misdemeanours: 3d for 'Henry Mattock, for scolding to extremity on Sunday without cause'; 6d for 'Richard Meadowes, for being absent when my Lord came home late, and making a headless excuse'; and 6d for 'Robert Verrell, for giving away my money'. Richard and Frances had a total of thirteen children, most of whom died young. The latter years of their marriage were marred by a family quarrel, which lasted for at least ten years. In 1655 the couple had agreed with Frances's brother that if he were to die without heirs, then the Cranfield estates should pass first to her, and then to her eldest son, Charles, Lord Buckhurst. However, in 1673 – just a year before his death – Frances's brother changed his will and left the estates directly to Charles, bypassing Frances. Richard and Frances took Charles to court successfully, but Frances's determination exceeded her husband's and not only did she fall out with her son, but her obsession with the lawsuit drove her husband to the brink of separation.

After Richard died in 1677, Frances continued to live at Knole, marrying Henry Powle in 1679, while their son Charles resided mostly at Court or at Copt Hall. Some of the silver in the King's Room dates from this period, including the silver table bearing the monogram FCD (for Frances Cranfield, Countess of Dorset).

The silver vases in the King's Room date from the 5th Earl and Countess of Dorset's time

THE 6TH EARL AND THE RESTORATION OF KNOLE

Charles Sackville had been born during the Civil War, probably at Copt Hall. By his late teens he was exhibiting all the characteristics of a Restoration rake. In 1662 he was one of five young men found guilty of the manslaughter of a tanner, whom they had mistaken for a robber; they were pardoned by the King. The following year he was indicted with two others for 'exposing themselves to the populace in very indecent postures' from the balcony of a brothel in Covent Garden, causing a riot in the process. According to the diarist Samuel Pepys, the Lord Chief Justice – when told that this was the same Lord Buckhurst who had been tried for another offence the previous year – 'asked if he had so soon forgot his deliverance that time, and that it would more become him to have been at his prayers begging God's forgiveness than now running into such courses again'. Once again, however, he was let off scot-free.

In 1667 Charles fell in love with the actress Nell Gwyn, with whom, according to Pepys, he 'kept merry house at Epsom' for a time. One of Nell's

(Left) Richard, 5th Earl of Dorset (1622–77), from the tomb of his son, Thomas (d.1677), by C. G. Cibber in Withyham church, Sussex, where generations of the Sackvilles are buried

Charles, 6th Earl of Dorset (1638–1706) in portly middle age; by Sir Godfrey Kneller

previous lovers had been the actor Charles Hart, and she is said to have referred to Sackville as her 'Charles the Second'. Two years later, she did in fact become the mistress of King Charles II (who, in the romantic merry-go-round of the Restoration Court, became her Charles the Third).

In 1674, however, Charles married a celebrated beauty, the Dowager Countess of Falmouth (whose portrait hangs in the Spangle Dressing Room). A series of his love letters to her survives, testifying to 'the violentest passion that eaver any body was capable of having'. By the time of her death in childbirth in 1679, this passion seems to have cooled, as one commentator observed:

With tame submission to the will of Fate,
He lugg'd about the Matrimonial Weight;
Till Fortune, blindly kind as well as he,
Has ill restor'd him to his Liberty;
That is, to live in his old idle way
Smoking all Night, and dozing all the Day.

In the year of his marriage, Charles's Cranfield uncle died, and he inherited Copt Hall and a fortune,

and the Cranfield title, Earl of Middlesex, was revived for him. Three years later, on the death of his father in 1677, he became 6th Earl of Dorset and inherited Knole. Thus began the assembly at Copt Hall (and later, at Knole) of the outstanding collection of 17th-century furniture, textiles and portraits that compensated for the losses of the Civil War and that are now on public display.

THE KNOLE COLLECTIONS

Charles went to France for his health in 1681, embarked on a string of casual affairs and resisted pressure from his mother, Frances, to get married again – 'I doe pasionatly Long to see you fixte,' she wrote to him. In 1685, however – in the tradition of his forefathers – he married an heiress, Lady Mary Compton, the seventeen-year-old daughter of the Earl of Northampton (her portrait hangs in the Ballroom). His grandson later wrote that Charles 'was during his whole Life, the Patron of Men of Genius, and the Dupe of Women'. He 'married three Times; but only one of these Marriages contributed either to his Honour, or to his Felicity.' This was it. He appears, at the age of 42, to have settled down to country life at Copt Hall and to have become increasingly uxorious; his wife bore him a son and a daughter (whose joint portrait hangs in the Ballroom).

He also appears to have revived his flagging public career. Charles Sackville had benefited from his friendship with Charles II. In 1668 he had been made a Groom of the Bedchamber, and in 1669/70 he had been sent to France as ambassador to the Court of Louis XIV. For his role in helping to negotiate the secret Treaty of Dover in 1670, he had been given the carved gilt table and candlestands now in the Cartoon Gallery. There were gifts from Charles II as well: annuities, grants of pieces of land and estates that had been forfeited by murderers and suicides, for example. Between 1680 and 1688, however, Charles Sackville was out of office at Court; and between 1685 and 1688, at least, out of sympathy with the new King, the Catholic James II, who was forced to flee the country after the Glorious Revolution of 1688–9.

The 6th Earl's moment came in January 1689,

when he supported the accession to the throne of King William III and his wife Queen Mary. As a reward, Charles was appointed Lord Chamberlain of the King's Household, in which capacity he supervised the domestic affairs of the monarch, ordering new keys for Queen Mary's apartments in Whitehall, ensuring that the Speaker's Chair in the House of Commons had a new velvet cushion, and arranging for the accommodation of the Court on its visits to the various royal palaces. He was also a member of England's first cabinet and one of several regents during the King's frequent trips to his native Holland.

One of the traditional 'perquisites' – or perks – of the Lord Chamberlain's office was that he could dispose of any furniture from the royal palaces – particularly Whitehall, Hampton Court and Kensington – when it was no longer required, on the death of a sovereign or simply when it was felt to be out of date. This is how the 6th Earl acquired the finest collection of Stuart furniture in the world. For example, the King's Bed, which had probably been made by Louis XIV's upholsterer to celebrate the marriage of the future King James II to Mary of Modena in 1673, was removed from Whitehall Palace after the death of Queen Mary in 1694; as was the matching suite of chairs and stools. An inventory that year describes the bed as 'of cloth of silver flowered with gold & lined with a silver fringe and feathers of red and white'. Similarly, the bed in the Venetian Ambassador's Room, together with the matching suite of armchairs and stools, was removed from Whitehall in 1695. Many other goods were acquired in the same way: the tapestries in the Spangle Bedroom and the Venetian Ambas-

The X-framed chair of state and the tapestries in the Spangle Bedroom were probably among the royal furnishings acquired in the 17th century by the 6th Earl or his grandfather, the 1st Earl of Middlesex, as perks of office

sador's Room; the brass locks in the Cartoon Gallery bearing William III's monogram; and the X-framed chairs of state flanked by footstools in the Brown Gallery – indeed, almost all the carved and upholstered pieces of furniture at Knole. There is, for example, a set of walnut chairs in the Brown Gallery with the initials WP (Whitehall Palace) stamped beneath the seats. As recently as 1995, a metal inventory brand, dated 1661, from Hampton Court Palace was matched precisely with a chair of state at Knole. Even the close stool in the King's Closet – a 17th-century royal lavatory or 'seat of easement' – had originally been used by the Stuart kings in Whitehall Palace.

Most of this furniture went first to Copt Hall, where it joined the collection already assembled by Charles's grandfather, Lionel Cranfield, 1st Earl of Middlesex. In 1701, however, Charles sold Copt Hall, and its contents – both the royal perquisites and the Cranfield chattels, including the family

The blue damask chairs in the Brown Gallery bear the royal stamp for Whitehall Palace, from where they were removed by the 6th Earl

portraits by Daniel Mytens and Van Dyck, and the copies of the Raphael cartoons that now hang in the Cartoon Gallery – were transferred in six wagon-loads to Knole.

Frances Cranfield had died in 1687, and her personal estate, including some houses on the Strand and the silver furniture she had acquired, had passed – after a brief legal squabble with her second husband's family – to her son, Charles. He also did some collecting and commissioning of his own: for example, the silver wall-lights in the King's Room, which bear the arms of Sackville and his second wife, Mary Compton; and, possibly, a few

of the Lely portraits now shown in the Spangle Dressing Room.

The rewards of high office were not confined to cast-off furniture. There were also substantial opportunities for profit from the sale of public offices and patronage at Charles's disposal – he received many letters from friends, relations and acquaintances requesting preferment and places at Court. One anonymous complaint, pinned – it is said – to the Lord Chamberlain's door, claimed:

If Papist, Jew or Infidel
　Would buy a place at Court:
Here Dorset lives, the Chamberlain,
　To whom you may resort.
Then come away, make no delay.
　Bring coin to plead your cases;
He'll turn the King's friends out of doors,
　And put you in their places.

Some of this money was paid for building works at Knole: for example, the wrought-iron gates in the garden wall that bear his cipher; the Cranfield coat of arms framed by swags of fruit and flowers on the parapet in the Stone Court (brought from Copt Hall); and the Sackville and Cranfield arms above the main gate on the west front.

But much was spent on entertaining, as well. The 6th Earl had a great reputation as a genial host. 'A freedom reigned at his table,' wrote his protégé, the poet and diplomat Matthew Prior, 'which made every one of his guests think himself at home.' This is confirmed by an account of his cellar for six months, which lists '425 gallons of red port, 85 gallons of sherry, 72 gallons of canary [a sweet wine], 63 gallons of white port and a quart of hock'.

Many of the beneficiaries of his lavish hospitality were men of letters. In countless dedications by sycophantic poets and place-seekers, he is referred to as the 'Maecenas' of his age. His monument in the Sackville Chapel at Withyham in Sussex bears an epitaph by the poet Alexander Pope, which is reproduced in the Brown Gallery:

(Left) Lionel Cranfield, 1st Earl of Middlesex (1575–1645); by Daniel Mytens (no. 196; Leicester Gallery). He was the father of Frances Cranfield, Countess of Dorset, and this portrait, together with the rest of his famous collection at Copt Hall, came to Knole in 1701

Sir Peter Lely's Cymon and Iphigenia *(Spangle Dressing Room) was acquired by the 6th Earl*

Dorset, the grace of Courts, the Muses' pride.
Patron of arts, and judge of nature, died.
The scourge of pride, tho' sanctify'd or great,
Of fops in learning, and of knaves in state.
Yet soft his nature, tho' severe his lays
His anger moral, and his wisdom gay.

Dorset himself was a minor poet, the author of a popular ballard called 'To all you ladies now at land', written in 1665 while on a naval expedition off the coast of Holland, and of some vicious contemporary satire. 'For pointed satire,' wrote his friend and contemporary, the Earl of Rochester, 'I would Buckhurst [Sackville] chuse; The best good man, with the worst-nature muse.'

As well as Matthew Prior, his favourite poets and playwrights included John Dryden, Thomas Otway, William Congreve, William Wycherley, Thomas Shadwell, whom he had made poet laureate, and the popular dramatist Thomas D'Urfey, whose portrait hangs in the Billiard Room. One splendid account of his generosity survives (in an early 19th-century account). One evening Charles suggested that he and his guests should each write a few lines in a competition that would be judged by Dryden. After due deliberation, Dryden announced Charles's contribution the best: the winning entry read: 'I promise to pay Mr John Dryden five hundred pounds on demand. Signed, Dorset.' 'I must confess', continued Dryden, 'that I am equally charmed with the style and the subject; and I flatter myself, gentlemen, that I stand in need of no arguments to induce you to join with me in opinion against yourselves. This kind of writing exceeds any other, whether ancient or modern. It is not the essence, but the quintessence of language; and is in fact, reason and argument surpassing everything.' Whereupon the company expressed 'a due admiration of his lordship's skill in fine writing'.

After the death of his second wife, Mary, from smallpox in 1691, Charles was – according to his grandson – 'extenuated by Pleasures and Indulgences and sinking under premature Old Age', a view corroborated by Kneller's portrait of a heavily jowled and fleshy figure swathed in a dressing-gown. In 1704, he 'married a Woman named Roche, of very obscure Connexions, who held him in a Sort of Captivity down at Bath, where he expired'. So worried were his family by his marriage to Anne Roche, a former housekeeper, that they considered having him put under some form of restraint and dispatched Matthew Prior to report on his state of mind. 'He drivels so much better Sense even now,' wrote Prior, 'than any other Man can talk, that you must not call me into Court, as a Witness.' There was no need to take any action, however, because the Earl died early in 1706.

CHAPTER SIX

THE 18TH CENTURY

Knole was, perhaps, at its most magnificent during the 18th century. In the first half of the 17th century, the Sackville family had all but lost Knole through personal extravagance and the effects of the Civil War. However, by the second half of the century, through a combination of canny marriages and the clever manipulation of influence at Court, they were in full possession of the house once more and were beginning to furnish it with the collection that visitors see today. Throughout the 18th century, there was new building – but it was generally ornamental rather than structural. And the family continued to collect, complementing the existing collection of Stuart furniture, paintings and textiles with objects that reflected the more eclectic tastes of the age.

THE 1ST DUKE

When Charles Sackville died in decrepitude in 1706, his eighteen-year-old son Lionel Sackville succeeded him as 7th Earl of Dorset. Lionel Sackville was in Italy at the time, where he had been sent by his maternal grandmother, the Dowager Countess of Northampton, to further his education and to escape the influence of his father and stepmother, Anne Roche. He had obviously not heeded a threat from his dying father to return immediately: 'i heare my Lady northampton has order'd you not to obey me, if you took any notice of what shee says to you i have enough in my power to make you suffer for it beyond what she will make amends for. . . . I expect you will come away by the next yocht.'

In 1709 Lionel brought his bride, Elizabeth Colyear – to whom he often refers in his letters as 'my dear Colly' – to Knole. As in the 17th century, the Sackvilles were not full-time residents. Like his father, Lionel enjoyed prolonged periods of public office, although he 'never had an opinion about

public affairs', according to Lord Shelburne. In 1714 he escorted George I from Hanover to England to assume the throne, and was rewarded with the Order of the Garter and by his reappointment as Warden of the Cinque Ports; in 1720 he was created the 1st Duke of Dorset. Above the fireplace in the Great Hall, there hangs a painting by John Wootton of the 1st Duke in ceremonial procession to Dover Castle in 1728, on yet another reappointment as Warden of the Cinque Ports.

The 1st Duke's political career was distinguished by two spells in Dublin as Lord Lieutenant of Ireland: from 1730 to 1737, and from 1750 to 1755. On one of these occasions he struck up a relationship with the actress Margaret 'Peg' Woffington. Some humorous verses survive, pastiching 'The humble Petition of Margt. Woffington, Spinster' to the Duke:

May it please your Grace with all Submission
I humbly offer my Petition . . .
I claim, my Lord, an annual kiss;
A kiss, by Sacred Custom due
To me, and to be pay'd by You:
But, least you entertain a doubt,
I'll make my Title clearly out . . .
It was as near as I can fix,
The fourth of April forty six;
(With joy I recollect the Day)
As I was dressing for the Play,
In stept your Grace, and at your back,
Appear'd my trusty Guardian Mac.
A sudden Tremor shook my Frame,
Lord, how my colour went and came!
At length, to cut my Story short,
You'd kiss'd me, Sir, Heaven bless you for't . . .
Since that, your Grace has never yet
Refus'd to pay the Annual Debt . . .

When the family were in residence at Knole, they were as lavish in their entertainment on the big occasions, such as Christmas, christenings, comings-

Lionel, 1st Duke of Dorset (1687–1765); by Sir Godfrey Kneller (no. 227; Ballroom)

of-age, weddings, funerals and royal visits, as their predecessors. For example, the 1st Duke calculated his expenses, including half an ox, four sheep and a calf, at £257, when entertaining the Prince of Wales, the future King George II.

For the first time in 100 years or so, improvements were made to the building at Knole. In 1723–4 the Huguenot artist Mark Antony Hauduroy decorated the Second Painted Staircase, between the Ballroom and the Reynolds Room, with grisaille trophies and arms. Around 1730 a Venetian window was added to the Venetian Ambassador's Room. In 1745 the clock and belfry were placed above Bourchier's gatehouse, crowning Knole's ancient glories with a more fanciful ornament of the modern age. And in 1748 a balustrade was built above the colonnade in the Stone Court.

For much of their time at Knole, the Dorsets had as their guests Lady Betty Germain, the widow of Sir John Germain, a friend and fellow-soldier of Elizabeth's father, General Colyear. Belying the slightly prim portrait that hangs in one of the rooms at Knole named after her, Lady Betty's letters – particularly to the satirist Jonathan Swift (whose portrait also hangs in Lady Betty Germain's Dressing Room) – are full of life and gossip. Her memory at Knole is preserved in her collection of oriental china and in the delicate scent of pot-pourri, still made from her recipe of 1750, that wafts through the state rooms.

On his deathbed in 1718, Sir John Germain had expressed the wish that Lady Betty remarry and have children who would eventually inherit Drayton, his Northamptonshire house. If, however, 'events should determine otherwise, it would give me great pleasure,' he told his wife 'to think that Drayton descended after your death to a younger son of my friend, the Duchess of Dorset – with the proviso that he change his name to Germain'.

Lionel and Elizabeth (whose portrait hangs in the Ballroom) had three sons. The eldest, Charles, eventually succeeded as 2nd Duke. The middle son, Lord John Sackville, was a keen cricketer and the organiser of the first match for which a full scorecard has survived – England v. Kent, on 18 June 1744. From his teens, his life was blighted

by bouts of severe depression until his death in Switzerland, where he had been exiled by his family, in 1765. According to a contemporary, Lord Edward Fitzmaurice, who saw him there in 1760, he lived upon 'a very poor allowance and but meanly looked after. He was always dirtily clad, but it was easy to perceive something gentleman-like in his manners, and a look of birth about him under all his disadvantages. His conversation was a mixture of weakness and shrewdness as is common in most madmen.'

THE COWARD OF MINDEN?

Lionel's favourite son was his youngest, Lord George. In family history, Lord George Sackville tends to be ignored or even disowned. Vita Sackville-West, in *Knole and the Sackvilles*, finds him 'an incongruity among the Sackvilles, a departure from type'. 'For some reason,' she concludes, 'Lord George never awakened my interest or my sense of relationship. He was a public character, not a relation.' This may have had something to do with his prickly, impatient character. According to one friend, there was 'a reserve and haughtiness in Lord George's manner, which depressed and darkened all that was agreeable and engaging in him. . . . His integrity commanded esteem, his abilities praise; but to attract the heart was not one of those abilities . . .'. Or it may have had something to do with the very public disgrace that disfigured his name.

Nevertheless, Lord George was one of the ablest members of his family, and the one who came closest to achieving the highest office. 'I do not conceive,' wrote Lord Shelburne, 'that any but the checks which stopped his military career could have prevented his being Prime Minister.' He served as a soldier from 1737, fighting in Flanders during the War of the Austrian Succession and in Scotland during the bloody suppression of the Jacobite Rising of 1745.

Lord George's problems began in 1759, when he was appointed Commander-in-Chief of the British troops in Germany, helping the Germans – under the supreme command of Prince Ferdinand of Brunswick – to defend Hanover against the French.

Lord George Sackville (1716–85); by Thomas Gainsborough (no. 251; Reynolds Room)

At the Battle of Minden in 1759, the British cavalry failed to capitalise on the success of the allied artillery in breaking the French centre. What might have been a rout was merely a victory. Was this because, in the fog of battle, Lord George had been confused by three sets of conflicting orders from Prince Ferdinand? Was it simply because he was slow in manoeuvring his cavalry squadrons into the line of attack? Was it because he had actively disobeyed Prince Ferdinand? Or, worst of all, had his conduct been cowardly?

Prince Ferdinand blamed Sackville and was backed by George II, who relieved Sackville of his command. Sackville was subjected to a vicious attack in the press and, in an attempt to clear his name, requested a court martial, despite the danger of a death sentence, if found guilty by two-thirds of the court. 'I am conscious of neither neglect nor disobedience of orders,' he claimed, 'as I am certain I did my duty to the utmost of my ability.' At the trial, Lord George was found guilty of disobeying

Prince Ferdinand, and pronounced 'unfit to serve his Majesty in any military capacity whatsoever'. But he was not sentenced to death, and this lenience – which infuriated George II, who described the disgrace as 'worse than death to a man who has any sense of honour' – cast some doubt on his culpability. It is a doubt shared by many historians today.

Lord George never really succeeded in shaking off this slur on his name. In 1768 he challenged a Captain George Johnstone to a duel in Hyde Park for impugning his honour. The protagonists exchanged two shots, one of which struck Sackville's pistol, and Johnstone later declared that he had never known a man behave better in a duel. In 1770 Sackville became Lord George Germain after inheriting Drayton from Lady Betty Germain, and five years later was rehabilitated when appointed Secretary of State for the American colonies. Despite the loss of the colonies in 1782, he emerged from the campaign with some credit and was awarded a peerage.

Lord George's disgrace at Minden was a great disappointment to his father, who, according to the poet Thomas Gray, 'went into the country some time ago and (they say) can hardly bear the sight of anybody'. The 1st Duke died in 1765, five years after his son's court martial.

THE 2ND DUKE

Lionel was succeeded by his eldest son, Charles, Lord Middlesex, who became 2nd Duke of Dorset. There is a full-length portait of him in the Ballroom by Franz Ferdinand Richter, dressed up as a Roman consul returning from the army. It was painted in 1738, probably to record the role he had played in a masque in Florence in 1737. Like many of his contemporaries, Charles went on the Grand Tour to Italy, first in 1731–3, and then in 1736–8. He was a member of the Society of Dilettanti, 'a club for which', according to Horace Walpole, 'the nominal qualification is having been in Italy and the real one, being drunk: the two chiefs are Lord Middlesex and Sir Francis Dashwood, who were seldom sober the whole time they were in Italy.' It was here that he developed his passion for Italian opera, which he

Charles, 2nd Duke of Dorset (1711–69), painted in masquerade dress while on the Grand Tour in 1731–2, by Rosalba Carriera

like his father, uncle and countless other young 18th-century aristocrats, he embarked on a Grand Tour of Italy, travelling to Rome, Naples, Florence and Venice. A notebook providing *An Account of the Number and Value of the Pictures, Busts etc.* records what he bought in Rome that year through the influential dealer and cultural go-between, Thomas Jenkins, and his great rival, James Byres, and in Venice in 1771 from Count Vitturi. His acquisitions included *The Virgin and Child with St Francis and St Jerome* attributed to the workshop of Francesco Francia, Teniers's *A Hurdy-Gurdy Player* and *Le Marchand de Ratafia*, and Garofalo's *Judith with the Head of Holofernes*, the last sent from Rome by Jenkins in 1775.

The 3rd Duke was the only member of the Sackville family to create a collection of his own, rather than merely commissioning specific portraits, or – as was the case with the 6th Earl – acquiring whole collections through inheritance or the perks of public office. Some of the smaller Old Master paintings from Italy, France and the Low Countries, which he acquired to complement the family portraits already at Knole, now hang in Lady Betty Germain's Dressing Room, while many of the larger ones are in the private apartments. But it was not always so. Paintings tend to migrate around a house over the centuries, reflecting the different tastes of successive generations. Many of the 3rd Duke's acquisitions, either directly from Italy or through his London dealer, would have had a greater prominence then than now, proclaiming to the world that however great his respect for his ancestors, he was a man of refinement too. He would have been delighted by one particular letter he received from the politician and writer Edmund Burke:

I who am something of a lover of all antiquities must be a very great admirer of Knole. I think it the most interesting thing in England. It is pleasant to have preserved in one place the succession of the several tastes of ages; a pleasant habitation for the time, a grand repository of what has been pleasant at all times. This is not the sort of place which every banker, contractor or nabob can create at his pleasure. I am astonished to find so many of your rank of so bad a taste as to give up what distinguishes them, and to

spent vast sums promoting on his return to London. He died in 1769, aged 58, 'having worn out', according to Walpole, 'his condition and almost his estate. He has not left a tree standing in the venerable old park at Knole.'

THE 3RD DUKE

Charles was succeeded as 3rd Duke of Dorset by his nephew, John Frederick Sackville (whose father, John, the cricketer, had died in 1765). The history of the family – and their mental health – appeared to be following the course prescribed by the old verses:

Folly and sense in Dorset's race
Alternately do run . . .

John Frederick was only 24 when he celebrated his succession with a feast 'at which sixty stone of beef, mutton and veal were consumed'. In 1770,

John Frederick, 3rd Duke of Dorset (1745–99); by Sir Joshua Reynolds (no. 255; Reynolds Room). The Duke was one of Reynolds's most generous patrons

adopt what so many can do as well or better than they. I would not change Knole if I were D of Dorset for all the foppish structures of this enlightened age.

The 3rd Duke was also a patron of contemporary painters, particularly Sir Joshua Reynolds, who became a close friend and whose funeral he attended as a pall-bearer in 1792. Many of the portraits he bought from Reynolds during the 1770s now hang in the Reynolds Room. Some of these are of literary and theatrical acquaintances, such as Oliver Goldsmith, Dr Johnson, Samuel Foote and David Garrick. There is also the fine portrait he commissioned from Reynolds of Wang-y-Tong, a Chinese boy who had caught his attention while in the service of an old schoolfriend on leave from the East India Company. The Duke took Wang-y-Tong into his own household as a page and had him educated nearby at Sevenoaks School. Presiding over them all is Reynolds's full-length portrait of the Duke. Here is the devastatingly handsome man, whom the Duchess of Devonshire regarded as 'the most dangerous of men ... for with that beauty of his he is so unaffected, and has a simplicity and persuasion in his manner that makes one account very easily for the number of women he has had in love with him.'

The 3rd Duke's mistresses included the courtesan Nancy Parsons, who had previously been the mistress of the Prime Minister, the Duke of Grafton, and with whom he went to Italy in 1770; Mrs Elizabeth Armistead, the daughter of a Methodist shoemaker; and Lady Betty Hamilton, both before and after her marriage to the Earl of Derby. Reclining voluptuously at the foot of the Great Staircase is a nude figure of a woman, who used to be described as 'a good friend of the family' by the guides at Knole. More precisely, she was a celebrated Italian ballerina and the love of the 3rd Duke's life.

Her name was Giovanna Zanerini, but she was better known by her stage name of Baccelli (and as Jannette by the 3rd Duke himself). She had caught his eye when dancing at the King's Theatre in the Haymarket, at a time when ballet was beginning to develop into an art form independent of the opera. By 1779 she was his mistress and living for long periods at Knole, where Shelley's Tower (a corruption of Baccelli) in the Inner Wicket is still named after her. Baccelli bore the 3rd Duke a son, also called John Frederick Sackville, who went to school in Sevenoaks before joining the army as a lieutenant; he died of a 'deadly fever' in Port-au-Prince in the West Indies in 1796.

The 3rd Duke's mistress, Giovanna Baccelli, is commemorated by this plaster statue at the foot of the Great Staircase

Knole from the north-east in the mid-18th century; by Hendrick de Cort (private collection)

COUNTRY-HOUSE CRICKET

Baccelli scandalised local society by appearing at a ball in Sevenoaks wearing the Sackville family jewels. But scenes of a touching domesticity also survive from the 1780s at Knole, including an account in Baccelli's name for a cricket bat and stumps for the young John Frederick. Like his father, the 3rd Duke was a keen cricketer:

For unlike the modern way
Of blocking every Ball at Play
He firmly stands with Bat upright
And strikes with his athletic Might;
Sends forth the Ball across the Mead,
And scores six Notches for the Deed.

At Knole he employed a small squad of professional cricketers, including the bowler 'Lumpy' Stevens, whose prowess was partly responsible for the introduction of the third stump. In the early days of cricket, the wicket consisted of only two stumps; however, in a match between Hambledon and Kent in 1775, Lumpy bowled several balls in succession straight through his opponent's wicket. When Hambledon played England at Sevenoaks in 1777, Vine ground, three stumps were used for the first time.

The 3rd Duke even tried to introduce the game to his former mistress, the Countess of Derby, and 'other ladies of quality and fashion', encouraging them with an essay which posed the immortal question: 'What is human life but a game of cricket?' Some of his contemporaries certainly believed that such an attitude summed up his own view of life. When he was appointed British Ambassador to the Court of Louis XVI in Paris in 1783, the *Whitehall Evening Post* commented: 'In the estimation of many people, the Duke of Dorset is the most extraordinary accomplished nobleman we have – at cricket, tennis and billiards his Grace has hardly any equal.' Less charitably, he was described in 1791 as 'a most admirable cricket-player – more cannot be said of him as he is not in possession of any brains.'

Baccelli accompanied the 3rd Duke to Paris for some of his posting there. He was a generous patron of the Paris Opera – his lifelong interest in music reflected at Knole in the portrait of the violinist Felice Giardini in the private apartments, in the mahogany double violin case bearing his monogram in the Cartoon Gallery, and in a number of musical scores that have survived. La Baccelli performed at the Opera herself, scandalising some by dancing 'with a blue bandeau on her forehead, inscribed *Honi soit qui mal y pense*' – this was the Order of the Garter that the 3rd Duke had received in 1788.

The round of balls, receptions and lavish entertainment came to an abrupt end with the French Revolution in 1789. The Duke scuttled back to England, turning back an English cricket team that had assembled at Dover *en route* for a match that he had arranged in Paris. The experience shocked him deeply and confirmed in him a deep-seated horror of the French and all things revolutionary. 'I hope you will not return by that vile country [France]', he wrote in a letter to Georgiana, Duchess of Devonshire in 1792, 'I begin to hate the name of the country as I lose having *any* opinion of *any* of the inhabitants. . . . We must *take care* or else democracy will gain ground.'

He was not in the best of health either. In 1785 he had suffered a small stroke: 'you hardly ever saw any Person more alter'd than he is, – he has a catching in his right Eye, as if he had had a paralytic stroke, and in order to conceal it he constantly carries a Handkerchief to his Face,' wrote one acquaintance to another. He was also beginning to suffer from the depression that had afflicted his father.

Nevertheless, he decided to settle down to a respectable marriage. Baccelli was pensioned off with £400 a year – 'The Duke of Dorset and the Baccelli have just separated, and she is said to have behaved very well,' reported one newspaper. She died in 1801 from a long illness, 'which she bore with the most exemplary resignation and with that sweetness of temper which rendered her so attractive in the days of her youth and beauty.'

In 1790 the Duke married the heiress Arabella Cope, who brought with her a dowry of £140,000. The statue of La Baccelli was banished to 'the Top of the Stairs next the Wardrobe', according to the inventory of 1799. Arabella bore the Duke three children, including a legitimate male heir, George. But contemporary accounts of the Duke's ill temper during the 1790s make rather dismal reading. The man who had been reported to spend around £11,000 a year while in Paris and who had gambled up to 1,000 guineas on the result of a single cricket match, was now worried about money – fretting massively when the painter John Hoppner won fifteen shillings off him at a game of casino at Knole.

The 3rd Duke died in 1799, his legacy to Knole a rich seam of legends, a great art collection and improvements to the estate. He had acquired more land around the house, had replanted the trees in the park, and had added fashionable touches such as the new hot-houses for growing pineapples and other exotic plants.

He was survived by his six-year-old heir, George, and by his wife, Arabella, whose contrasting portraits hang at Knole – by Hoppner in 1790 (in the Reynolds Room) and some thirteen years later, by Vigée-Lebrun (in the Ballroom). In her memoirs, Mme Vigée-Lebrun recalls a visit to Knole, presumably when the Duchess was sitting for her:

The first time we met for dinner, the Duchess said to me: 'I'm afraid this will be terribly boring for you: you see we never talk at dinner.' I reassured her on this point, saying that I was used to this since I had eaten alone for many years. She must have been very

The heiress Arabella Cope (1769–1825) married the 3rd Duke in 1790; by Elisabeth Vigée-Lebrun (no. 222; Ballroom)

entrenched in this habit for during dessert, her son [the 4th Duke], then aged about eleven or twelve, came over to her and spoke very briefly to her; eventually she dismissed him without the slightest mark of affection. I could not help recalling what I had been told about the English – they care little for their children once grown, and only love little babies.

During the early 19th century, when the 4th Duke was still a minor, some alterations were made to the house by his mother and her second husband, Lord Whitworth: for example, an Orangery with large Gothick windows that faces the garden on the south side; and an arched window beneath the clock-tower that gives a Gothic character to the Inner Wicket.

THE 4TH DUKE

A family Bible records that the 4th Duke had been born on 15 November 1793, and that one of his godfathers was George III: 'He was inoculated and had the Small Pox in Dec. 1794. He had the Measles in 1796, the Scarlet Fever in Nov. 1797, the Hooping Cough in 1803, the Chicken Pox in 1804, the Mumps in 1809.' He was an industrious pupil, according to his obituary: 'The hours of study were employed in reading the Bible, in learning his Grammar, in translating Aesop's Fables from Latin into English, and the Psalms from English into Latin; in reading a portion of the Universal History, in repeating a short Poem, and in other useful occupations'. All this before the age of eight, when he went to Harrow School. There he was befriended by the poet Byron, who later addressed a poem to him recalling their attachment.

The handsome young man in the full-length portrait by George Sandars in the Ballroom came of age on 15 November 1814. There was a big party at Knole with bonfires. Within a few months, he was dead – his spine crushed by a falling horse in a hunting accident in Ireland, where Lord Whitworth was then Viceroy. Arabella continued to live at Knole until her death in 1825, with the house eventually passing to her daughters. The title meanwhile, passed to Lord George Germain's eldest son, Charles, who lived at Drayton and became 5th Duke of Dorset. The historian Sir Nathaniel Wraxall lamented:

George, 4th Duke of Dorset (1793–1815), who was killed in a hunting accident shortly after this portrait was painted by George Sandars (no. 223; Ballroom)

The very name of Sackville appears to be near extinction, the present Duke of Dorset [Charles] being unmarried, and Mr. Germain [Lord George's younger son] without male issue. . . . Even the dukedom itself seems to be deprived of its greatest ornament, and to be half extinguished by the loss of Knole. . . . That venerable pile, where the Earls and Dukes of Dorset has resided in uninterrupted succession for more than two centuries . . . it is highly probable will be transferred to the Earls of Delawar, in consequence of a will which, whatever legal validity it may possess, militates against every feeling of justice and propriety.

CHAPTER SEVEN

THE 19TH AND 20TH CENTURIES

The will to which Sir Nathaniel Wraxall was referring in the quotation on p. 85 was the settlement made on Arabella's death. In 1825 the Sackville estates were divided between Arabella's two daughters, Mary and Elizabeth. Mary, who had married the Earl of Plymouth in 1811, received Knole and the Kent estates, while Elizabeth, who had married George West, the 5th Earl de la Warr, in 1813, inherited Buckhurst and the Sussex estates.

After her mother's death, Mary lived at Knole with the Earl of Plymouth (after whom the lodge at the north-west corner of the park is named) until his death in 1833. In 1839 she remarried, and brought her second husband, William Pitt, Earl Amherst, a former Governor-General of India, to Knole. Earlier in his career, Amherst had been sent as British Envoy to China and had returned with a rare breed of golden pheasant, *Phaisanus Amherstiae*, which he introduced to England. Several of these birds were housed in one of the seven courtyards at Knole, which is still known as the Pheasant Court, while others lived in an aviary in the park, beside the Gothic Revival building called the Bird House.

Knole and Buckhurst, the Kent and Sussex estates, were temporarily reunited on Mary's death in 1864. Mary had no children by either marriage, and her estates passed to Elizabeth for her younger sister's lifetime. In 1843, by royal licence, Elizabeth had added the Sackville name to her husband's, thereby creating the name of Sackville-West for her descendants who still occupy parts of the house.

Through a complicated sequence of wills, codicils and royal patents, Elizabeth intended that her eldest surviving son, Charles, should inherit the Buckhurst estates (along with her husband's de la Warr title), while the second surviving son, Reginald, should inherit Knole after her death. When her husband died in 1869, Charles duly became 6th Earl de la Warr and owner of Buckhurst. Elizabeth

died the following year, and Reginald Sackville-West inherited Knole – but only for three years. In 1873 Charles died without issue, and Reginald became the 7th Earl de la Warr. Mortimer, the next son down, now claimed that – on his elder brother's succession to the earldom – the ownership of Knole and the Sackville estates should shift to him.

Mortimer took his claim to court, and won. In 1874 he sued Reginald for having removed valuable heirlooms from Knole during his three-year occupancy, and won again. Such litigiousness – so typical of the Victorian era – was to be a feature of Knole and the Sackvilles for the next 40 years. It also earned for Mortimer a place in family mythology as a rather disagreeable man, who had, by the end of his life, succeeded in falling out with most of his relatives.

RIOTOUS AND TUMULTUOUS PROCEEDINGS

Mortimer also fell out with the local community. In June 1884 a dispute over public rights of way led to 'riotous and tumultuous proceedings', when a crowd of at least 1,500 people invaded the park at Knole and besieged the house. Behind the dispute lay the changing ways in which people viewed and visited great country houses and estates in the mid-19th century.

In 1874 some 10,000 people visited Knole House. This was a very different phenomenon from the country-house visiting of the 18th century, when a handful of connoisseurs – or simply curious gentlefolk – were occasionally shown around a house by the housekeeper. The opening of Hampton Court Palace to the public in 1839 had initiated a new age of country-house visiting. Some owners were disturbed by the numbers of the new tourists and the inevitable rise in petty vandalism that followed –

The visit of the Prince and Princess of Wales to Knole in the summer of 1866

and attempted to limit them by instituting fixed visiting hours and admission charges. Others, like Mortimer, simply shut their doors. Knole House was effectively closed to the general public until after Mortimer's death in 1888.

Nevertheless, the number of visitors to the house was small compared with visitors to the park. Although the park was – and is – privately owned, the paths across it had come to be seen as rights of way and the park itself as a public amenity. Sevenoaks was only an hour by train from London, and by the 1880s there were 30 trains every weekday from London and fifteen on Sundays. As well as improvements in the rail network, people had more free time – what with Saturday half-holidays and the new Bank Holidays. And, as a result, Knole became for the first time a popular destination for a day trip to the countryside from the crowded capital.

The park was also treasured by the inhabitants of Sevenoaks themselves. The population of this market town had doubled over the previous 20 years, rising to 8,000 in 1881. Local residents liked to stroll in the park; mothers wheeled their children in prams along the paths; people from nearby villages rode on horseback or in carts across the park to do their shopping in town; and everyone, particularly shop and hotel owners, benefited from the passing weekend trade that the park attracted.

Mortimer had had enough. He complained about people 'galloping promiscuously about the park', and in 1883 he had posts placed across the main gate to prevent horses, and even prams, from entering. There was a public outcry. On the night of 18 June 1884, a crowd of people from Sevenoaks broke down the posts across the entrance and, singing 'Rule Britannia', marched on the house where they deposited the posts at the main door. The next evening they entered the park again, surrounded the house, smashed a few windows, and shouted abuse at Mortimer before proceeding to the Fawke Gate, at the far end of the park. There they forced the gate open and ceremonially rode back and forth through the entrance.

It had been a largely peaceful procession. Men dressed as women wheeled prams symbolically through the park, contributing to the midsummer carnival spirit. But Mortimer was alarmed and asked the Chief Constable to increase the number of policemen stationed at Sevenoaks; by the second evening, there were 114 of them. Even after the situation had calmed and while a compromise acknowledging the public rights of way was being made, Mortimer felt threatened and left Knole temporarily, to live in the Grand Hotel, Scarborough, and at St Leonard's in Sussex.

The 'riot', as Mortimer described it, marked a turning point in the history of Knole. Newspaper articles at the time implied that the privileges of wealth could no longer be manipulated at will, at the expense of the traditional rights of the people: privilege, it was widely believed, now entailed some sense of responsibility towards the local community. In the same year as the riot, the Third Reform Act extended the vote to millions more, further eroding the monopoly of political power previously enjoyed by the aristocracy. In economic terms, too, the agricultural depression of the 1870s and 1880s, with cheap food from the Americas and Australia flooding the European market, forced down land rents and values, threatening the owners of landed wealth still more.

Many landowners started to break up their estates and to sell them off. Mortimer may have felt beleaguered by the erosion of aristocratic privilege and power, but the Sackvilles at Knole survived (despite a fire in 1887, which gutted areas of the Stable Court). Indeed, in ceremonial terms at least, Mortimer's position was enhanced: in 1876 he had been created Baron Sackville of Knole for his decades of service in Queen Victoria's household.

Mortimer died childless in 1888 and was succeeded as 2nd Lord Sackville and owner of Knole by his younger brother, Lionel, a diplomat. Mortimer's death coincided with Lionel's recall in some disgrace from his position as British Minister in Washington. Lionel had been tricked into expressing an opinion as to which of the candidates in a forthcoming presidential election would best represent Britain's interests. Contravening all

REMOVEING THE FIRST OBSTRUCTION AT ENTRANCE TO KNOLE PARK

On the night of 18 June 1884 a group of people from Sevenoaks tore down the posts which Mortimer Sackville had put up in an attempt to close the park to visitors. The 'riotous and tumultuous proceedings' were reported in the Penny Pictorial News on 28 June

protocol, Lionel wrote a letter recommending the Democrat candidate; the Republicans (who had devised the trick question in the first place) then published Lionel's response. There was an outcry. 'It was ironical', someone later remarked to Vita Sackville-West, 'that your grandfather of all people, the most taciturn of men, should have been sacked for expressing himself too freely.'

Lionel was unable to take possession of Knole immediately because – once again – there were complications over a Sackville will. Mortimer had thrown one posthumous spanner into the works by leaving much of his personal estate (he was only a life-tenant of Knole itself) to Queen Victoria's four maids of honour. Whether this provision was an extraordinary act of spite towards his relatives or whether, as Vita suggested, 'he had private reasons for wishing to benefit one of them, and hit on this method of doing it without singling her out into scandalous publicity,' it was contested by Lionel – and settled out of court.

THE ROMANCE OF THE SACKVILLE PEERAGE

In the summer of 1889 Lionel eventually took up residence at Knole, accompanied by two of his illegitimate daughters, Victoria and Amalia. As a young man in Paris in 1852, Lionel had fallen in love with Josefa Durán, a Spanish dancer also known as Pepita. The daughter of a barber and a door-to-door clothes saleswoman from Malaga in Spain, Pepita was recently estranged from her husband, Juan Antonio Oliva. In 1858 she gave birth to her first child, Maximiliano Leon Jose Manuel Enrique Bernardino (known as Max for short) and, over the course of a nineteen-year relationship that lasted until Pepita's death in 1871, the couple had four more children: Victoria, Flora, Amalia and Henry. At first, their affair was conducted around the diplomatic capitals of Europe, but in 1865 Lionel installed his growing family in the Villa Pepa in Arcachon in south-west France, where he would visit them from postings in Madrid and Paris.

When Lionel was posted to the United States in 1881, his daughter Victoria had joined him in Washington as his social hostess, and on his return to England, she effectively became mistress of Knole. By the end of her first year in England, she had met and married her first cousin, young Lionel Sackville-West who – in the likely event of Victoria's father failing to produce any legitimate heirs – was heir to Knole. Through this union – one that was initially blessed by a great deal of passion on both sides – Victoria made her position as mistress of Knole more than a temporary one. 'Jour de ma vie!' she wrote in her diary on her wedding day, 17 June 1890, repeating the rather strange family motto adopted by Mortimer in 1876.

Their daughter, Vita, who was born in 1892, had many wonderful memories of growing up at Knole at the turn of the century, with her father, mother and grandfather. She remembered her grandfather with great affection; 'old Lionel', she wrote, 'never did say anything; he had his own occupations, which included reading right through Gibbon every other year and whittling paper-knives from the lids of cigar-boxes. He liked the garden, where two Demoiselle cranes and a French partridge with pink legs followed him sedately about, but for the rest he was quite content to leave everything to Victoria [Vita's mother].'

Victoria was a woman of formidable energy. As mistress of Knole, she had some 24 servants working in the house. At the top of the hierarchy were the butler and the housekeeper, Mrs Knox, and at the bottom were the footmen, laundrymaids and the housemaids, who got up just before 6 every morning to polish the grates and to carry brass cans of hot water up to the bedrooms. There were 20 people working for Mr Stubbs, the head gardener, in the pleasure gardens and in the walled kitchen garden; four blacksmiths in the forge; a gamekeeper, Mr Findlay; and carpenters, foresters and labourers on the home farm, which supplied milk, eggs, butter and cream to the big house.

Victoria also set about making Knole more comfortable. It was on her initiative that a telephone was installed in her father's bedroom in 1891, that bathrooms with hot running water gradually replaced the brass cans, that central heating was introduced, and that the house was fully electrified by 1902. She even decorated one room with a wallpaper composed rather laboriously of postage stamps.

By the turn of the century, Knole was a magnificent place in which to enjoy a lavish weekend house party. From the living-rooms on the south front, guests could flow through French windows out into the garden. It was in front of one of these that the Prince and Princess of Wales were photographed with friends and family on a visit in July 1898. This was the house and period immortalised as Chevron in Vita Sackville-West's novel *The Edwardians*.

But although Knole may have appeared as grand as it had been since the 18th century, and although the estate may have seemed self-sufficient, the agricultural depression of the 1880s continued to eat away at the family fortunes. The estate that Lionel had inherited in 1888 consisted of some 8,000 acres, yielding £11,250 a year – a relatively modest income with which to maintain such a house. On top of that were the costs of Victoria's entertaining and home improvements, and Lord Sackville's continued attempts to support his and Pepita's other children, including setting Max and then Henry up as farmers (rather unsuccessfully) in South Africa.

Selling assets was an obvious strategy for many families at the time; and the Sackvilles, for example, sold the portrait of Baccelli by Thomas Gainsborough in 1890; it is now in the Tate Gallery. Some families succeeded in diversifying out of land and into other business interests, while other families managed to marry newly wealthy American heiresses. But Victoria, who was almost as good at making money as she was at spending it, adopted a less conventional strategy.

Victoria was particularly successful at accepting money from male admirers. One of these was the immensely wealthy Sir John Murray Scott, described by Vita as an 'enormous man, six-feet-four in his stockings, he weighed over twenty-five stone, and for all my efforts as a child I never could get a five-foot measuring tape to meet round the place where his waist ought to have been.... Perpetually flapping a large silk handkerchief to keep away the flies, he rolled and billowed along on disproportionately tiny feet.' Seery, as he was known, constantly 'lent' Victoria large sums of

Victoria, Lady Sackville (1862–1936) in fancy dress costume for the Devonshire House Ball in 1897

(Right) The Cartoon Gallery in 1897; by Charles Essenhigh Corke

money – totalling up to £100,000 over the course of their friendship – and even bought a house for her and Lionel in Mayfair. It was a tempestuous relationship – more an *amitié amoureuse* than a full-blown affair – and Victoria was, in turn, charming and then tiresomely capricious, wildly extravagant in her fondness and then utterly grasping. When Seery died in 1912, he left Victoria £150,000: the capital was to go to Knole, while Victoria could enjoy the income. He also left her the contents of his house in Paris, which comprised a substantial part of the famous Wallace Collection. This she immediately sold for £270,000 to a French art dealer, soon spending the proceeds.

The money could not have come at a better time. Victoria's father had died in 1908, and on top of death-duties, which had been introduced in 1894, there were legal costs of around £40,000 resulting from yet another lawsuit. Over Knole in the 1890s had hung the cloud of a disputed inheritance. The family knew that, on old Lionel's death, his son

Henry, whose farming venture in Africa had finally failed, would claim that he was the legitimate owner of Knole and the heir to the peerage. If Henry could prove that Pepita had never been married to Oliva, then there was always the possibility that Lionel had, in fact, been secretly – and legitimately – married to Pepita. This case relied on the fact that whereas Max had been registered at birth as the son of Pepita and Oliva, and Victoria as the 'fille de père inconnu' – which disqualified them – Henry and the two younger girls had been registered as the legitimate children of Lionel and Pepita. Lionel, on the other hand, always claimed that he had condoned this form of words simply to placate Pepita.

Throughout the late 1890s and early 1900s, there had been a certain amount of skulduggery. It seemed that Henry's accomplices had tampered with the parish register in a church in Madrid, in an attempt to discredit the record of Pepita and Oliva's marriage; and a private investigator was despatched

On 16 February 1910 Lord and Lady Sackville, with their daughter, Vita, returned to Knole after winning their High Court action over the disputed Sackville peerage

to Spain by the Sackville family to investigate. There had also been dreadful scenes at Knole, when Henry – threatening suicide – had turned up at Knole to see his father, and had been ejected by the servants.

After old Lionel's death in 1908, Victoria and her husband (now 3rd Lord Sackville) left Knole in the hands of the family trustees until the question of the inheritance was settled. In February 1910, the case opened in the High Court in London. 'The Romance of the Sackville Peerage', as it was described, attracted massive press coverage on both sides of the Atlantic, with its heady mixture of ancient wealth and modern manners, high life and low life. Henry's petition was dismissed within six days, and he killed himself four years later.

On 16 February, Lionel and Victoria returned to Knole in style. Unlike Mortimer, Lionel's father had been a popular local figure. The couple rode through Sevenoaks in a horse-drawn victoria. At the top of the hill, a triumphal arch welcomed them home, the horses were led away, and the victoria was then pulled by members of the local fire brigade through the park to Knole. 'An abominable nuisance' is how Lionel described the proceedings.

LORD AND LADY SACKVILLE

Only three years later, the Sackvilles were involved in another high-profile lawsuit. In 1913 the Scott family contested Seery's will, claiming that Lady Sackville had exercised undue influence over Seery in his declining years. Two of Britain's most outstanding barristers represented the parties: F. E. Smith for the plaintiffs, and Sir Edward Carson for Lady Sackville.

During the course of this *cause célèbre*, considerable doubt was cast on the morals of the Sackville family. Lady Sackville was accused of having attempted to seduce Seery's youngest brother, Walter, and Lord Sackville was quizzed about his rounds of golf with his ladyfriend, Lady Constance Hatch. On 7 July, the case ended in victory and vindication for Lady Sackville. But the revelations highlighted the fact that Lionel and Victoria, whose marriage had begun with so much promise and passion, had begun to go their separate ways.

Lionel took his responsibilties as a country gentleman seriously: he was Vice-Chairman of the Kent County Council, a Deputy Lieutenant and Justice of the Peace, and commander of the West Kent Yeomanry: all of which activities bored Victoria. He had also embarked on a long affair with a singer, Olive Rubens, whom he was later to install with her complaisant husband in a flat at Knole. Finally, in August 1914, with the departing words to his wife of 'Well, dear, I am afraid I must be going now', Lionel left for the war with his regiment — to fight in the Dardanelles, Palestine and France.

Victoria, on the other hand, had continued to attract a string of distinguished male admirers, including the sculptor Auguste Rodin, Max Beerbohm, J.P. Morgan, Rudyard Kipling, Lord Kitchener, William Waldorf Astor, and a Swedish diplomat called Baron Bildt. In one of many supposedly money-making schemes, she also started an interior decorating shop, called Speall's, in Mayfair.

By the end of the war, Lionel and Victoria's marriage had broken down irretrievably. In 1919 Victoria moved to a house she had bought in Brighton; and for the next 17 years, until her death in 1936, her life became one of increasing eccentricity. Vita chronicled her mother's later years with a mixture of adoration and exasperation. Victoria's money-making schemes continued. In order to repair one of several houses she had bought, she sent a circular letter to all her friends and acquaintances, asking them to contribute enough cash to buy a tile for her Roof of Friendship fund; and was extremely irritated when the painter William Nicholson took her at her word and sent a tile wrapped up in a paper

parcel. Her meanness — she once wrote to Vita on lavatory paper filched from the ladies' room at Harrods, 'Regarde, comme ce papier prend beaucoup mieux l'encre que Bromo' — was matched by great generosity and extravagance. She might leave £1,000 in cash in a taxi, or on a whim buy her daughter a chain of emeralds and diamonds: equally capriciously, she might demand them back, claiming that Vita had stolen them.

Knole was probably a greyer place without her. In 1921 the house was advertised as available for rent, along with several other major country houses, including Leeds Castle, Blickling and Corsham Court. It never was let, but the very possibility is typical of a time when many owners believed that the country house was no longer viable. Between 1918 and 1921, some 7 million acres (around a quarter of England) was sold, causing

Vita Sackville-West, painted at Knole in 1910, when she was eighteen, by Philip de Laszlo (Sissinghurst Castle)

The Times to complain that England was 'changing hands'; and many houses were pulled down and their features – panelling, staircases, fireplaces and so on – sold off to builders and architectural scrap merchants.

Lionel, however, lived on at Knole until his death in 1928. Although Vita was effectively a Sackville twice over – her parents had been first cousins and her grandfathers brothers – she did not inherit Knole, the house she loved with what she described as an 'atavistic passion'. The title and the house were entailed to pass through the male line, to her father's younger brother Charles and then to her cousin Eddy. 'Sissinghurst and St Loup are my spiritual homes,' she later wrote, 'and of course Knole, which is denied to me for ever, through "a technical fault over which we have no control", as they say on the radio.'

This technical fault – her gender – caused her much resentment. Although her uncle Charlie gave her a key to the garden, Vita hardly ever visited Knole again – partly because she disliked Charlie's second wife, Anne. But she could still describe it vividly from memory almost 20 years later, when the National Trust commissioned her to write the guidebook to the house. And she still felt any slight to Knole most intensely. 'I always persuade myself that I have finally torn Knole out of my heart,' she wrote when Knole was damaged by a bomb in 1944, 'and then the moment anything touches it every nerve is *à vif* again. I cannot bear to think of Knole wounded, and me not there to look after it and be worried about it.'

Vita's uncle, Major-General Sir Charles, 4th Lord Sackville, was a professional soldier, who had served with distinction in India, in South Africa during the Boer War, and in the First World War; after retiring from the army, he was Lieutenant-Governor of Guernsey and Alderney from 1925 until 1929, when he took up residence at Knole. Almost immediately, he was forced to sell certain family heirlooms, including the tapestries in the Chapel. The house parties continued, however (one of Anne's guests was her fellow American, Mrs Wallis Simpson, the future Duchess of Windsor), and cocktails were served at Knole for the first time. Photographs of Charlie show a figure of great

The music critic and writer Eddy Sackville-West (1901–65) succeeded as 5th Lord Sackville in 1962; by Graham Sutherland

inter-war elegance: co-respondent shoes, and the distinctive yellow waistcoat that had earned him the nickname 'Tit-Willow' from his students at Sandhurst.

KNOLE AND THE NATIONAL TRUST

The Second World War finally brought an end to this era of country-house living – just as the First World War had threatened to do. In June 1940 James Pope-Hennessy described a visit to Knole in almost elegiac terms: 'We walked in the great dark gardens in the evening light with wide turf alleys and rhododendron flowers, and urns on pedestals; and the house and the elms; but there was only an illusion of peace and the previous tranquil world, and the whole ordered landscape seemed quivering with imminent destruction.'

Many of the house's more valuable contents were removed to a slate quarry in North Wales for safe keeping. But as threatening to Knole as the war itself were the rising taxes. 'At this moment', Charlie wrote to his son Eddy in 1940, 'we are all under the influence of the budget ... it is the end definitely for such houses as Knole. I do not see how anyone in any country will be able to buy objets d'art. The death duties on top of Income and Surtax will make it impossible to pay the wage bills & maintenance of the building etc.' He feared that it would be the last summer 'in which flower gardens of any kind can be kept up'.

Such worries about the future of Knole had encouraged Charlie to enter into discussions with the National Trust in 1935. These negotiations continued throughout the war until, in 1946, the Sackville family finally handed the house over to the National Trust with an endowment towards its maintenance. The family retained possession of the park and many of the contents of the house, and were granted a 200-year lease on various private apartments within the house.

In 1946, on a visit to Knole, James Lees-Milne, the Historic Buildings Secretary of the National Trust, had described the 'piles of dust under the chairs from worm borings. The gesso furniture too is in a terrible state. All the picture labels want renewing; the silver furniture cleaning; the window

mullions mending.' So began 50 years of repairs, restoration and conservation, in which hardly a stone has been left untouched – at a cost in special government grants of over a million pounds.

Charlie died in May 1962, and was succeeded as 5th Lord Sackville by his son Eddy, the first peer in four successions since the title was created in 1876 to succeed his father. But Eddy, novelist, critic, musician, confirmed bachelor and aesthete, had never cared that much for Knole (or, indeed, for his step-mother Anne). 'Ireland suits my temperament,' he had told the *Daily Mail* gossip columnist on his purchase of a house there in 1956, 'I prefer it to that big place in Kent.' In 1964, the year before his death, he wrote:

Living at Knole now is (to me, at any rate) extremely disagreeable – particularly in summer, when it is all but impossible to walk outside the garden walls without stepping on a prone figure. It is like living in the middle of Hyde Park! However, my cousin Lionel luckily loves the house enough to put up with this (and other) features of the modern world, none of which I can abide.

Agonising over his decision as 'inheritor of a glorious palace the burden of which he had been forced by a disobliging new world to shift on to the shoulders of an alien organization', Charlie had told James Lees-Milne 50 years ago that no Sackville after Eddy would live at Knole. In fact, Charlie's nephew Lionel moved with his large family into part of the house in 1961, and on Eddy's death in 1965 became 6th Lord Sackville. In 1967 Lionel's younger brother Hugh moved with his equally large family into another part of the house, and – as agent for the National Trust as well as for the family – supervised much of the National Trust's restoration programme. Knole is now inhabited by more members of the family than at any time in the past four centuries.

BIBLIOGRAPHY

The Sackville Papers are on deposit in the Centre for Kentish Studies in Maidstone.

ALSOP, Susan Mary, *Lady Sackville*, London, 1978.

BRADY, J.H., *Visitors Guide to Knole*, 1839.

BRIDGMAN, John, *History and Topographical Sketch of Knole*, 1817.

CLIFFORD, D.J.H., ed., *The Diaries of Lady Anne Clifford*, Stroud, 1990.

COLEMAN, John, 'Reynolds at Knole', *Apollo*, cxliii, April 1996, pp. 24–30.

COLEMAN, John, 'Mysterious Blooms', *Country Life*, 6 March 1997, pp. 78–81 [Flower paintings in the Cartoon Gallery].

CORNFORTH, John, 'Stitching in Time', *Country Life*, 25 November 1982, pp. 1651–3.

CORNFORTH, John, 'Glow of Gold Brocade', *Country Life*, 6 August 1987, pp. 64–5.

DRURY, Martin, 'Italian Furniture in National Trust Houses', *Furniture History*, xx, 1984, pp. 38–42.

DRURY, Martin, 'Two Georgian Chairs of State and a State Canopy at Knole', *Furniture History*, xxi, 1985, pp. 243–9.

DRURY, Martin, 'A Diplomat's Prize', *Country Life*, 3 October 1991, pp. 54–5.

EDWARDS, Ralph, 'A Set of Carved and Gilt Furniture at Knole and its Restoration', *Connoisseur*, cxlv, April 1960, pp. 164ff. [Furniture in Venetian Ambassador's Room].

EINBERG, Elizabeth, *Gainsborough's Giovanna Baccelli*, London, 1976.

FAULKNER, P.A., 'Some Medieval Archiepiscopal Palaces', *Archaeological Journal*, cxxvii, 1970, pp. 140–6.

GLENDINNING, Victoria, *Vita*, London, 1983.

GORE, St John, 'Paintings of the Early Sackvilles', 'Paintings bought by a Duke', *Country Life*, 7, 14 October 1965, pp. 886–8, 972–4.

HARRIS, B., 'Charles Sackville, 6th Earl of Dorset, Patron and Poet of the Restoration', *Illinois Studies in Language and Literature*, xxvi, nos. 3–4, 1940.

HUSSEY, Christopher, 'The Spell of Knole', *Country Life Annual*, 1961, pp. 28–36.

JACKSON-STOPS, Gervase, 'The 6th Earl of Dorset's Furniture at Knole', *Country Life*, 2, 9 June 1977, pp. 1495–7, 1620–2.

JOURDAIN, Margaret, *Stuart Furniture at Knole*, London, 1952.

KILLINGRAY, D., 'Riots, "Riot" and Ritual: the Knole Park access dispute', *Rural History*, v, no. 1, 1994, pp. 63–79.

LAING, Alastair, *In Trust for the Nation*, 1995, pp. 22–3, 197, 232.

LEES-MILNE, James, *People and Places*, London, 1992, pp. 166–83.

MACKESY, Piers, *The Coward of Minden*, Harmondsworth, 1979.

MACKIE, Samuel Joseph, *Knole House: Its State Rooms, Pictures and Antiquities* [1858].

MANDLER, Peter, *The Fall and Rise of the Stately Home*, London, 1997.

MARLOW, Louis, *Sackville of Drayton*, London, 1948.

PASTON WILLIAMS, Sara, *The Art of Dining*, London, 1993.

PHILLIPS, C.J., *History of the Sackville Family*, 2 vols., London, 1929.

SACKVILLE, Lionel, Baron, *Knole House: Its State Rooms, Pictures and Antiquities*, Sevenoaks, 1906.

SACKVILLE-WEST, Vita, *Knole and the Sackvilles*, London, 1922.

SACKVILLE-WEST, Vita, *Pepita*, London, 1937.

SIMON, Robin, 'When Revolution Stopped Play: John Frederick Sackville, 3rd Duke of Dorset, Cricket Patron', *Country Life*, 18 April 1985, pp. 1006–7.

STEWART, Linda, *Across Miry Vale*, diss., 1992.

TINNISWOOD, Adrian, *A History of Country House Visiting*, Oxford, 1989.

TIPPING, H. Avray, 'Knole of the Archbishops – I', 'Knole of the Earls – II', 'Knole of the Dukes – III', *Country Life*, 25 May, 1, 8 June 1912, pp. 772–87, 826–39, 862–73.

WELLS-COLE, Anthony, *Art and Decoration in Elizabethan and Jacobean England*, London, 1997.